SARDAR PATEL

Winner of the Atta Galatta-Bangalore Literature Festival Book Prize for Best Children's Fiction 2023, and the Binod Kanoria Children's Book Award 2023 in the Young Adult category, Mallika Ravikumar is a lawyer-turned-writer. An MA in Ancient Indian History and Culture, she was the curator and chief content writer for the Government of India's National Virtual Library of India portal on Sardar Vallabhbhai Patel's life and legacy.

Mallika also loves learning about trees, conducting tree walks and creating videos about trees on her YouTube channel, 'Tree Talk with Mallika Ravikumar'. You can find out more at www.mallikaravikumar.com and reach her on Instagram at @mallika.ravikumar.

SARDAR PATEL

MAN OF IRON * WORDS OF STEEL

50 Inspiring Stories from the Leader's Life

MALLIKA RAVIKUMAR

hachette INDIA

First published in 2025 by Hachette India
(Registered name: Hachette Book Publishing India Pvt. Ltd)
An Hachette UK company
www.hachetteindia.com

1

ISBN 978-93-5731-351-3

Hachette Book Publishing India Pvt. Ltd
4th & 5th Floors, Corporate Centre
Plot No. 94, Sector 44, Gurugram – 122003, India

Typeset by Manmohan Kumar, Delhi

Printed and bound in India
by Thomson Press India Ltd.

MIX
Paper | Supporting responsible forestry
FSC www.fsc.org FSC® C010615

To

Tatha,

For introducing me to history as you'd lived it.

Contents

Introduction xi

1. LIGHTING THE FIRST TORCH 1
Make your own way
2. GRIT AND GUTS 6
What hurts us may heal us
3. THIS TOO SHALL PASS 11
Put others first
4. AGAINST THE CURRENT 17
Break free of blind faith
5. AN INVISIBLE POISON 21
Examine your biases
6. UNCHARTED, UNDAUNTED 26
Hold power accountable
7. SAY YES TO THE UNKNOWN 30
Step out of your comfort zone
8. SILENT VALOUR 35
Lead from the front

9. THE CROSSOVER 39
Actions speak louder than words
10. MIRROR BEFORE WINDOW 47
Before judging someone, walk a mile in their shoes
11. STORMS PASS, BONDS STAY 51
Balance your boundaries
12. QUICK ON THE COMEBACK 56
Harness the power of wit
13. GOING THE WHOLE HOG 61
Fight it out, then move on
14. NO OFFENCE 72
You can be assertive without being aggressive
15. REALITY CHECK 76
Test the waters before jumping in
16. LOVE OVER EGO 81
Don't cash in on grief
17. HOUR OF RECKONING 86
Persist and you shall prevail
18. SERMON OF THE BUFFALOES 91
Find humour in the mundane
19. PLAIN HONESTY 96
Choose facts over foolery
20. IRONCLAD 99
Contentment is a state of mind
21. SARDAR FOREVER 103
Earn your honours
22. THE WIT WITHIN 108
Laugh through life's troubles

23. NO IMPOSITION 113
Be stern, not strict
24. RAW AND REAL 116
Call a spade a spade
25. STANDING TALL 119
Respect yourself first
26. UNBREAKABLE 123
Don't play the victim card
27. PATIENCE PAYS 127
Sometimes, restraint is the best response
28. THE SHOW GOES ON 132
Do business without bitterness
29. FOREVER YOUNG 137
Keep alive the child within
30. THE COMMON TONGUE 145
Speak to be understood
31. MONEY MATTERS 149
Stay practical, yet principled
32. STANDING FIRM 154
Place principles over personalities
33. BENDING WITHOUT BREAKING 158
Let go of rigidity and embrace change
34. ANCHOR DOWN 161
You can be firm, yet gentle
35. ROOM TO DIFFER 167
Disagreement does not mean disrespect
36. GOAL OVER ROLE 170
Go beyond the rat race
37. WHEN IDEALS CLASH 175
Sometimes, compromise is the best solution

38. DREAM BIG 179
You can pull off the impossible
39. NO PLACE FOR YES-MEN 189
Seek challengers, not cheerleaders
40. ONE NATION, MANY VOICES 194
Look beyond the narrow lens
41. A FRESH START 198
Everyone deserves a second chance
42. TRUTH WITHOUT TAINT 202
Follow reason over emotion
43. UNAPOLOGETICALLY LIGHT 210
Don't take yourself too seriously
44. EMPATHY FIRST 214
Busy hands, open heart
45. SPEAK UP 219
Face the bully
46. NO GRUDGES 224
Be magnanimous; choose grace
47. BREAK THE CHAIN OF REVENGE 226
Payback does no good to anybody
48. ABILITY OVER ANCESTRY 234
Courtesy counts
49. RECONSTRUCTION, NOT RETRIBUTION 237
Let bygones be bygones
50. LETTING GO 244
Accept the inevitable with grace

A Note from the Author 253
Acknowledgements 255

Before we begin

WHO WAS SARDAR PATEL AND WHY DOES HE MATTER?

Sardar Vallabhbhai Patel was the key architect of modern India. Without him, the map of India would not have looked like what it does today. Instead, it may have looked something like this.

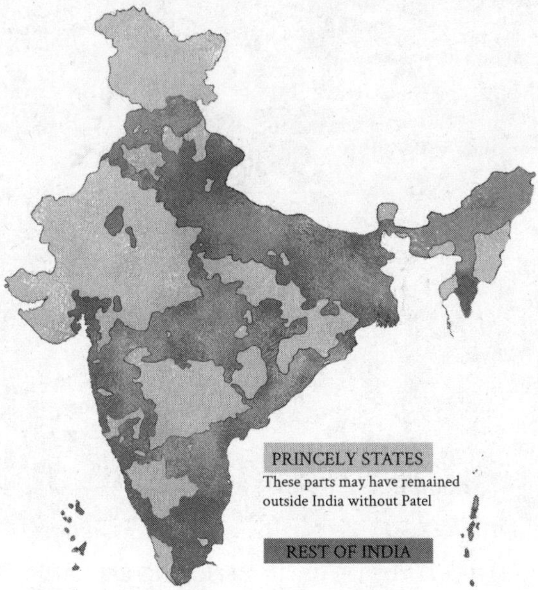

INDIA COULD HAVE HAD A FRACTURED, FRAGMENTED MAP HAD IT NOT BEEN FOR SARDAR PATEL

But for Sardar Patel, India may have been a country with disconnected portions of territory, including gaping holes comprising other nations and even bits of Pakistan within her borders! (Chapter 38 will give you a glimpse into how

THE STATUE OF UNITY DEPICTING SARDAR PATEL IS THE TALLEST STATUE IN THE WORLD

Sardar Patel pulled off this monumental feat of stitching the nation together against all odds.)

It is because of this that 31 October (Sardar Patel's birth anniversary) is celebrated in India as National Unity Day.

Befittingly, a statue of the architect of modern India is the world's tallest statue. Named the Statue of Unity for Patel's contribution to uniting India, the colossal monument, measuring 182 feet, towers over the River Narmada, near Kevadia in Gujarat.

> ‘The story of his great life…is a great story… history will record it in many pages and call him the builder and consolidator of the new India.’
>
> JAWAHARLAL NEHRU, FIRST PRIME MINISTER OF INDEPENDENT INDIA

WHY WAS HE CALLED SARDAR? WAS HE A CHIEF OF SOME KIND?

Yes and no.

Vallabhbhai Patel was born in 1875 to a family of farmers. His mother's name was Ladba, and his father was Jhaverbhai. He was born in Nadiad and grew up in Karamsad, located in Gujarat.

He studied to become a lawyer (depending on books borrowed from friends) and qualified as a barrister from England after saving up twice over for the trip and crossing many hurdles. (You can read about that dramatic saga in Chapter 3.)

It was his dream to become a wealthy lawyer. He worked hard towards fulfilling that ambition and managed to reach his goal.

However, after years of struggle and success, there came a twist in the tale. Patel threw away all that he had earned and walked away. Why? What for? (Chapter 5 will tell you more about that.)

Soon, the path he desired became the one he abandoned. The new road he took led him to many new adventures and challenges. He became one of the most important leaders of India's freedom struggle and left a mark in many ways on the nation's future. It was during this journey that the prefix *Sardar* got added to his name.

Sardar was not a title he was born with. Nor was it an honour bestowed upon him by the government. It was given to him by the people of Bardoli in Gujarat in 1928 because they saw in him their leader, their chief. It was a title that he earned with love and respect from people at the grassroots because of his stellar work (Chapter 21 has more on that). And the title stuck. Ever since, he was known as Sardar Patel.

This book is not a typical biography.

It does not tell you everything about Sardar Patel from the day he was born to the day he died.

Instead, it shines the spotlight on fifty stories from his life – dramatic episodes that offer a glimpse into his extraordinary life, along with takeaways from his journey, that you can use to shape your own.

> That there is today an India to think and talk about is very largely due to Sardar Patel's statesmanship and firm administration.
>
> RAJENDRA PRASAD, FIRST PRESIDENT OF INDEPENDENT INDIA

BORN READY

Patel plucked 31/10/1875 out of thin air when asked to write down his date of birth for his matriculation exams in 1897. As for many born in that era, there is no clear documentation showing the date of his birth. It is likely that 31 October is not really his birth anniversary. 'I have to bluff when asked how old I am,' Patel would often say, in keeping with his jovial nature. 'When I have to say it on oath, I add the word "approximately".' Despite his serious appearance, Patel was quite a prankster. (Chapters 12, 15, 22, 29 and 43 will give you a glimpse into this witty and humorous side.)

1

LIGHTING THE FIRST TORCH

Make your own way

Vallabhbhai Patel was born in 1875 in the town of Nadiad in Gujarat to Jhaverbhai and Ladba. Jhaverbhai was a small landowner and cultivator who often took young Vallabhbhai with him to the fields. Right from childhood, Patel had grand ambitions. With his family being neither wealthy nor influential, Vallabhbhai would have to chart his own way to pursue his dreams.

'No, Vallabh,' Jhaverbhai turned down his son's request. 'We have already sent your older brother to the English school at Nadiad. Your going will be a burden on your uncle there.'

Disappointed to hear his father's words, young Vallabhbhai buried his head behind his book, sitting by the single kerosene lamp in their simple home. His older brother Vithalbhai had been sent to study at the English school in Nadiad, about 20 kilometres from his hometown of Karamsad. He too wanted to go.

'At the bazaar I heard someone say that a new school is going to be opened here,' said Ladba, Vallabhbhai's mother, as she rolled out the bedding for the night. 'They mentioned that a private English school up to the third grade is starting—'

'Only up to class three?' cut in Jhaverbhai. 'But Vallabh is too old for that.'

'That's alright…' Vallabhbhai tugged at his father's arm, his ambition to be a great man someday glinting in his eyes. Growing up in Karamsad, Vallabhbhai had not had much exposure to the world outside. But this much he knew – becoming a lawyer was a pathway to success, and in order to become a good lawyer, he would need to know English. His Gujarati-medium village school would not get him there; he'd have to go beyond. 'I'm ready to start again.'

Ladba and Jhaverbhai stared at each other for a moment. A simple homemaker and sturdy farmer, neither had any

YOUNG VALLABHBHAI DISPLAYS EXTRAORDINARY FORESIGHT AND COURAGE FROM HIS BOYHOOD DAYS

formal education. But Jhaverbhai recognized the daring spirit in his boy, for he himself had dared to be different. Back in 1857, he had travelled all the way from Gujarat to fight alongside the Rani of Jhansi in India's First War of Independence. Seeing that their son was determined to get an English education, the parents got Vallabhbhai enrolled in the new school, where he went to complete his third grade when he was seventeen years of age!

His determination unyielding, Vallabhbhai then moved to the town of Petlad, about 15 kilometres from Karamsad, which also had an English school – but only until grade 5.

Walking to his school in Petlad each morning, Patel found a particularly large boulder that obstructed people's way. Stopping to do something other passers-by had not done, young Vallabhbhai went down on his knees and tried loosening it by shaking it out of the mud into which it was jammed.

'What are you doing that for?' asked his classmates who were walking with him to school.

'This rock can injure people – it's an obstacle in our way,' replied Patel.

'So what?' shrugged a friend. 'Just leave it be.'

'What? No!' Patel shot back, putting all his strength into pulling out the stone, as the others looked on. 'If something is creating a problem, it has to be set right.'

Focused on getting an English education, after completing two years of school in Petlad, Patel then shifted to Nadiad to continue with grade 6.

At his new school, Vallabhbhai encountered a particularly harsh teacher, who often hit students with a cane. One day, the teacher fined a student to punish him. When the boy was unable to pay up the amount, the teacher shouted at him and ordered him to leave the class.

Seething that his classmate had been treated so rudely, Vallabhbhai decided to take on the teacher for hurting the pride of a small boy. First, he staged a walkout from class, taking all his classmates out with him. Then, he decided to go further.

After classes were over for the day, Patel organized a meeting of all the students in the school. 'To show our protest, we shall launch a strike – a mass walkout,' he addressed the students. 'No student shall enter school.'

For the next three days, the students camped in a local resthouse, refusing to leave till action was taken against the excessive measures of the errant teacher. A fine organizer, Patel had taken care to arrange for food and water for all the children to enable them to hold out as long as needed.

Giving in to pressure from parents and townspeople, the headmaster finally called Vallabhbhai to meet him.

'No student will be unjustly punished in future,' the headmaster assured Patel. 'You have my word.'

The settlement in place, Patel then called off the strike, and the students returned to class.

As intolerant of fraud as he was of injustice, Patel once organized a boycott against another teacher who ran a stationery business, and compelled students to buy books and pencils only from him. The boycott was so successful that ultimately the teacher had to give up his side business.

Yet, Patel's love was as fierce as his opposition. When another teacher, an earnest man of little means, decided to run for the municipal elections and found himself repeatedly snubbed by his wealthy and arrogant opponent, Patel decided to back him to win the race.

'Whoever loses the election,' the opponent had declared confidently, 'will have to shave off his moustache.' (The moustache was seen as a symbol of masculine pride.) Campaigning extensively for his teacher, Patel ensured his teacher won a resounding victory in the elections. Then, along with about fifty of his classmates, Vallabhbhai went to the home of the opponent, taking a barber along. 'Step out of your house now and get your moustache shaved,' they demanded.

As it happened, these early lessons in battling destiny and power with daring and determination would hold Vallabhbhai in good stead in the years to come. Life was to throw many challenges his way, and Patel would not shy away from taking them head-on.

> What inspiration, courage, confidence and force incarnate Vallabhbhai was! We will not see the likes of him again.

C. RAJAGOPALACHARI, CONGRESS LEADER AND FREEDOM ACTIVIST

2

GRIT AND GUTS

What hurts us may heal us

It's the year 1900. Vallabhbhai is twenty-five years old. He is studying for the District Pleader's exam so that he can practice law without taking the longer route of completing an LLB degree, as he has family responsibilities and must begin earning. Deciding to study along with his friends for the exam, he stays at the haveli of his friend Kashibhai Desai in a village called Bakrol. During his time there, he develops a painful boil in his armpit, because of which he can't concentrate on his studies.

'Tch!' Patel winced, flapping shut the heavy book he had borrowed from a senior lawyer to prepare for the Pleader's examination, which was to take place in a week's time. 'I'm fed up of this boil.'

'Have patience, Vallabh,' said his friend Chhotabhai as he turned up the kerosene lamp. 'It will heal soon.'

'No...' Vallabhbhai bit his lip. 'It is constantly distracting me. I must do something to get rid of it. There must be a remedy...'

'I have an idea,' said Kashibhai Desai, whose home in Bakrol they were camping in. 'But it can be very painful.'

'Please tell me,' Patel pleaded with his friend. 'I just want to end this misery.'

'There is a barber...' began Kashibhai hesitantly. 'People in the village call for his help in such situations. From removing teeth to puncturing boils, he has a solution for all these problems.'

'Well then, let's try that,' said Patel.

'But think it over,' Kashibhai said, grimacing. 'His method is not going to be easy or pleasant.'

'Nor is this!' Patel stood up. 'Let's go right away,' he said, leading the way down the narrow steps of the haveli from the room on the second floor.

'Lakshmi Ram...' Kashibhai called out to the cook downstairs, 'Vallabh has a painful boil and needs help. Could you ask the barber to help him?'

'Madha Rat?' asked Diwaliba, Kashibhai's sister-in-law, who was pickling chillies in the foyer.

'He is an expert at curing such things,' said Lakshmi Ram.

'But it will be terribly painful,' interjected Amu Mian, the house help who was hanging up clothes to dry in the courtyard. 'He will burst the boil with an iron spike.'

'I am not afraid of that,' replied Patel without flinching. 'Please bring Madha Rat here... I want to get on with my studies. There's very little time left for the exam.'

'Very well,' shrugged Diwaliba, sensing Patel's anguish. 'Amu, go and fetch Madha Rat. Tell him to get all the tools he needs.'

In a few minutes, Amu Mian returned with Madha Rat, the barber of Bakrol village. Setting down the metal box in his hand, Madha Rat called Patel to the courtyard. 'Let me see the boil.'

Patel went out to the sunlit patio, his friends following closely behind him.

'Ohhhh!' Madha Rat exclaimed as he examined the boil from different angles. 'Hmmm... Ooooooh... Shhhhh...'

'What is it?' asked Diwaliba as Lakshmi Ram and Amu Mian stood by anxiously. 'Can you pierce it?'

'It is rather large and badly infected.' Madha Rat screwed up his nose as he opened the box and brought out a large iron poker. 'Come this way...' He led Patel towards a wood fire at one end of the courtyard, where a pot of water was boiling. 'Let me warn you,' he said. 'This is going to hurt.'

So saying, Madha Rat pushed one end of the iron poker into the flames, and in a few minutes, it became red-hot.

'Now, I'm warning you again,' Madha Rat began, 'this is going to be—'

'Oh, just get on with it, will you?' Patel gritted his teeth.

Madha Rat stepped closer and held up Patel's arm. As he brought the poker near Patel, he stopped and winced, his eyes partly shut as he held back from delivering the painful blow.

'What are you waiting for?' Patel rebuked the barber. Then he grabbed the lance from his hand and plunged it into the boil to puncture it.

Madha Rat gasped, as did the rest, surprised at Patel's daring act.

This, though, was not a one-off incident. Patel's fearlessness and resilience were on display yet again a few years later, during his stay in England, where he went to become a barrister.

Patel developed blisters on his leg after he fell in the bathroom. But the doctors there could not diagnose the problem, as they had no experience of it. Looking up a book on tropical diseases, Patel identified it as guinea-worm disease, a condition caused by drinking contaminated water. Despite several days of treatment involving two operations and the removal of some veins, the doctors failed to take out the worm completely. The infection spread, and his condition worsened, until one day, the surgeon suggested that if Patel wanted to save his life, he would have to get his leg amputated.

Refusing to accept such a fate, Patel then decided to consult another doctor, at which time a twist in the tale presented itself.

'You may get alright,' the second doctor said, 'if you are operated upon without chloroform.'

'Not a problem.' Patel's decision was swift as always. Of course, he knew that without chloroform, he would be conscious through the agonizing procedure. 'I can endure any amount of pain,' he said confidently. 'Please go ahead with the surgery.' True to his words, not once did he moan during the operation, which was ultimately successful in ridding him of the problem.

Marvelling at Patel's endurance, the surgeon who had operated upon Patel said that he had never seen a patient with such Herculean strength.

> 'I saw Vallabhbhai Patel for the first time this morning…uncompromising, but more of a man than most of the Indian politicians I have met.'

VICEROY LORD WAVELL, AFTER HIS MEETING WITH PATEL IN JANUARY 1946

3

THIS TOO SHALL PASS

{ Put others first }

After completing his matriculation in 1897, Patel decides to become a lawyer. But he can neither afford university nor wait six years to finish his LLB. After taking the District Pleader's exam, he opens a small office in Godhra to begin his practice. He soon becomes known as a fine criminal lawyer but quickly realizes that if he is to be more successful, it would help if he qualified as a barrister from England. So, in 1910, he decides to go to London. But his fate meets with a cruel twist – not once but several times over.

Resting his elbows on his desk, young Vallabhbhai went through his accounts once again. Despite having set up his practice only five years ago, and in spite of the plague having wrecked the region, he had saved a sufficient amount. It finally seemed like there was enough to give flight to his dreams.

Reaching out for paper and pen, he began writing a letter to the travel agency, Thomas Cook and Son, requesting a passage to London on the next available ship. Over the next few days, he would have to make several other arrangements, apart from breaking the news to his young wife, Jhaverben. His daughter Mani was two and his son Daya just one; they were too young to understand that their father would be away for three long years.

A few weeks after his preliminary preparations got underway, his brother Vithalbhai came to visit him at the office, flapping a large envelope in hand. 'I…received this…' He set down the packet.

Eyes locking momentarily with his brother, Vallabhbhai picked up the open envelope. It was from Thomas Cook and Son, and had been addressed to V.J. Patel. He knew what it contained.

Because his brother had the very same initials as him, the travel documents had gone to him instead. 'I am your elder,' Vithalbhai cleared his throat, 'I should go to England first.'

Dumbstruck, Vallabhbhai stared at his brother.

'I have not mentioned this to anyone…but I have also been keen to go to London to study further and become a barrister.' Vithalbhai pursed his lips. 'And as the elder one, I should go first.'

Vallabhbhai sat back on his chair, turning the packet over in his hands.

'You can postpone your going,' Vithalbhai said, shrugging. 'Go after I return…'

Vallabhbhai looked up at his brother. The postponement he was asking for was at least three long years. But without batting an eyelid, he nodded. 'Alright,' he said. 'You can go in my place. I have saved some money for the trip – you can have that as well.'

Over the next few days, Vallabhbhai helped his brother prepare for the journey, even accompanying him to Bombay* to bid him farewell. Among other things, he arranged for Vithalbhai's wife Diwaliben, to stay at his home, taking on the financial expenses of his brother's family during his absence. And then without a complaint, he got back to his work as a district pleader in Borsad – cross-examining witnesses, preparing pleadings and arguing cases. Starting from scratch, he once again began saving up to study in England.

As the months rolled on, disputes arose between his wife Jhaverben and Vithalbhai's wife Diwaliben, causing much tension at home. To avoid friction, Vallabhbhai asked his wife to move to her parents' house for a while, as he considered it inappropriate to reproach his sister-in-law while his brother was away.

In 1908, Vithalbhai returned from England after two and a half years. But Vallabhbhai's time to realize his dreams had not yet come.

Patel's wife Jhaverben had fallen very sick and was suffering from acute intestinal problems. To get her treated by a competent doctor, Vallabhbhai took his wife to Cama Hospital in Bombay.

* *Now Mumbai*

'She requires a surgery,' the doctor informed them, 'but we cannot operate now. She is too frail, and we must wait for her health to improve.'

'I understand,' said Vallabhbhai. 'I need to return to Anand for my client's case. I am in the middle of conducting a murder trial. But as soon as you decide to go ahead with the operation, please let me know so I can come to Bombay immediately.'

After making certain his wife was comfortable, Vallabhbhai left for Anand. But soon thereafter, the doctor decided to operate upon Jhaverben as her condition had suddenly worsened. The operation was a success, and a telegram was sent to Patel conveying the good news.

Yet, the very next day, Jhaverben passed away.

Another telegram was sent to Vallabhbhai conveying the tragic news. Patel was in court then, in the middle of his case. The murder trial was at a critical stage, and his client, the accused, was a well-known man. As a messenger came into the courtroom bearing an urgent telegram for Patel, he was in the middle of cross-examining one of the most important witnesses in the case. Patel read the telegram. His heart nearly stopped. He read the words again. His mouth fell open. *How could this be?* But the very next moment, he composed himself, without showing any trace of his shock to the world outside. If he paused at this juncture and sought an adjournment, the case could go against his client.

With a heavy heart, Patel folded the telegram and put it into his coat pocket. Then, controlling his own grief, he continued cross-examining the witness, putting his client's interests ahead of his own emotions. It was only after finishing his arguments that he shared the sad news. As it happened, his client was acquitted of the charge.

Distraught, Vallabhbhai found himself a single parent at just thirty-three years of age. His children, Mani and Daya, were just five and four. His dream appeared to be slipping away.

Before the family could recover from that blow, they were struck by yet another – Diwaliben fell seriously ill. Putting off all thoughts of pursuing higher studies in England, Vallabhbhai devoted himself to the family. He brought his sister-in-law to Borsad for further treatment. But, in 1910, she too passed away.

Heartbroken, Patel was in a quandary. He was responsible for two very young children and his window of opportunity to pursue his dream was closing fast. Patel heard that the rules were about to change: those without an LLB degree were soon going to be disallowed from taking the Bar Exam. Moreover, his going would pave the way for a better future for Mani and Daya; they too could study in England when they grew older.

For the sake of his future and theirs, Patel made the difficult decision. Leaving his children with Miss Wilson of Queen Mary's School in Bombay, where they were to be taught to speak good English in order to prepare them for a life in England later, he left for London in August 1910, after entrusting his home and practice to his younger brother.

After several hiccups, Vallabhbhai finally set off to pursue his dream. In London, he completed his studies in less time than usual after obtaining an exemption of two terms due to his stellar performance. In June 1912, after standing first in the first division, he returned to India and went on to have a successful legal career in Ahmedabad.

> I came from a middle-class family. … I was told that only if I could get seven to ten thousand rupees, I would be able to proceed to England. … I realized finally that if I wanted to go to England, I had to earn the money myself. I, therefore, studied very earnestly for my Law Examination and resolved firmly to save sufficient money for a visit to England.

VALLABHBHAI PATEL, IN A SPEECH DELIVERED IN 1921

4

AGAINST THE CURRENT

{ Break free of blind faith }

Despite being born to a traditional conservative family of farmers, Patel broke free of conventional customs that he did not approve of. Whether it was the practice of giving dowry, making wasteful expenditures on laborious rituals, child marriage or caste taboos – he raised his voice against age-old irrational habits and beliefs, even when it came to taking a stand against members of his own family.

In 1914, Vallabhbhai Patel's father, Jhaverbhai, passed away. As was customary after the death of a person, Narsibhai, who was Vallabhbhai's older brother, decided to invite community members for a meal on the thirteenth day after the death.

'These rituals are completely pointless,' said Vithalbhai, Vallabhbhai's eldest brother. 'Why must we waste money like this?'

'I agree,' nodded Vallabhbhai, seconding his brother. 'Such customs only increase the burden on the bereaved family.'

'What nonsense you two talk,' Narsibhai reprimanded his younger brothers. 'This is an age-old practice. Who are you to question it?'

'So what?' Vithalbhai argued back. 'So what if it is an old custom? If it doesn't make sense, we should discard the practice.'

'If you want to do something in Bapu's name,' Vallabhbhai intervened between his two brothers, 'why not use the money for a good social cause instead of spending it wastefully on a community meal?'

'You both have lost your minds,' an enraged Narsibhai chided his younger brothers, leading to a fiery exchange between both sides. A few years ago, Narsibhai had suffered a financial crisis. Refusing to let him mortgage family ornaments, Vallabhbhai had reached out to him, saying, 'Your debt is my debt... Give me the names of your creditors so I can relieve you as quickly as possible.' Narsibhai had not forgotten the timely aid given by his younger brother. Even so, his suggestion to break age-old practices, particularly customary rituals surrounding their father's death, came as a rude shock.

'Well, if you two do not cooperate and contribute to the ceremony'—Narsibhai gave an ultimatum—'you will have to give up your share in our father's ancestral property. You will not get a single penny.'

Vithalbhai and Vallabhbhai exchanged quiet glances. Simmering down, they nodded. Surrendering their share in their father's property, they both remained absent during the ceremony held on the thirteenth day.

In another instance, Patel expressed his disapproval of conservative social customs through his sardonic wit. Once, he found himself in the middle of an animated discussion at the engagement ceremony of a relative.

'How much dowry should we ask for?' an elderly relative was discussing with another.

'Our boy is a prize catch. We must not settle for anything less than 5,000 rupees.'

'I say we ask for more,' whispered another, as all eyes turned to Patel for his view.

'Why are you so worried?' Sardar snapped, enraged at the discussion among elders in his community. 'Why don't you just put the groom up for auction?'

It left everyone too stunned to say anymore.

He had, after all, refused outright to accept dowry at his own son Dahyabhai's wedding in February 1925. In fact, he had gone one step further still, refusing to hold a celebration or feast of any sort, preferring instead a simple ceremony at Gandhi's ashram.

The bride, Yashoda, was from Virsad, a village that his kinsmen in Karamsad had a feud with. For decades, there had been no marriage between people of the two villages, so Patel's choice of a bride from Virsad for his son was bitterly opposed in his village. Keen on setting an example to end petty squabbles, Patel went ahead nevertheless, asking Gandhi to officiate at the wedding.

About a decade later, he repeated the gesture, backing the wedding of his niece Vimla with a boy from Virsad.

'Forget all distinctions such as *high* families and *low* families...' Patel would urge the people of Karamsad. 'All are children of the same God.'

> I do not believe in any caste or community. The whole of India is my village and men of all communities are my friends and relations.

SARDAR PATEL, SPEAKING TO PEOPLE IN HIS HOMETOWN, KARAMSAD, IN 1942

5

AN INVISIBLE POISON

Examine your biases

In 1916, Vallabhbhai Patel is a well-to-do barrister with a successful legal practice in Ahmedabad. Dressed in a fine suit, felt hat and shining shoes, he speaks with an air of superiority, smokes expensive cigars, sends his collars to be laundered in Bombay and plays bridge at the Gujarat Club every evening. He dreams of amassing great wealth. Ten years later, however, he is a completely transformed man. He is dressed in simple khadi, a handspun dhoti and plain chappals, having devoted his whole life to the national cause – freedom from colonial rule.

'Where are you going?' Patel asked his friend Mavlankar as he sipped his tea under the hand-pulled punkha swinging above their heads. Seated on the veranda of the Gujarat Club, he was eager to get on with the next game of bridge, but his partner seemed to be abandoning the game table suddenly and turning his attention to the courtyard below, where a crowd was beginning to gather. 'Why have you got up?'

'Look there!' Mavlankar leaned over the balustrade to catch a glimpse of the special guest who had been invited to speak at the club that evening. 'His name is Gandhi,' he said, pointing to the frail figure entering through the gate.

'Bah!' grunted Patel. 'Forget him – let's play...'

'I hear he's a lawyer from South Africa,' said Mavlankar. 'Have you met him?'

'I have no time for such people,' scoffed Patel, throwing a glance of disdain at the barely clad Gandhi in the lawn below. Acutely conscious of his status and position, Sardar was puzzled by Gandhi's dress and mannerisms. *What sort of England-educated barrister went about dressed like that? And why were so many people thronging to listen to this man anyway?*

'Come along,' a young man came hurrying down the veranda. 'Gandhi is here to address us...'

'Go away!' Patel shouted him down. 'We don't want to listen to your Gandhi!'

Casting another derisive look at the visitor below, Patel couldn't help but laugh at the odd man and his unusual speech. 'I don't understand his brilliant ideas,' he said, reaching for his cigar. 'What do truth and love have to do with fighting colonial injustice and serving the public?'

'Oh...so you think the public will be served by playing bridge at the club, is it?' tittered a rebuking voice from the other end of the corridor.

With a sigh, Patel got up to leave. But the thought continued to bother him.

Over the next few months, Patel began to notice how his friends and acquaintances – intelligent people he respected and admired – teacher D.B. Kalelkar, writer Swami Anand and advocate K.G. Mashruwala – were smitten with Gandhi and his message. His friends Narhari Parikh and Mahadev Desai – competent lawyers for whom Patel had the highest regard – had been swept away by Gandhi's energy. His neighbour Mavlankar, his friend Harilal Desai – they all kept going back to hear him repeatedly. *What was drawing all these people to Gandhi?*

Despite his scepticism, the forty-two-year-old Patel decided to give the forty-eight-year-old Gandhi his patient ear and quiet attention. Months rolled on; weeks of listening and observing. At the Provincial Political Conference of the Gujarat Sabha at Borsad, Patel saw Gandhi insisting that Lokmanya Tilak and Muhmmad Ali Jinnah, both fiery lawyers and tall leaders of the Indian National Congress, speak not in English but in their native languages. In those times, when every political conference began with pledging loyalty to the King of England, Gandhi began the meeting on a very different note. He held up the loyalty resolution and tore it up.

Excitement coursed through Patel's veins to see a man of such courage. His days of brushing off Gandhi and cynically dismissing his ideas were firmly behind him. Something was beginning to stir inside him.

When he learnt more about Gandhi's transformation over time, from living as a barrister in South Africa to dressing in simple garments, travelling third-class on trains and addressing ordinary people in Gujarati – it amazed him and moved him. Vallabhbhai felt he too could change.

And then came a definitive moment in May 1917 when Gandhi pulled off a spectacular victory in Champaran, Bihar. By getting ordinary indigo cultivators to challenge the might of the British administration, Gandhi's defiance electrified the atmosphere of rebellion in the country, sweeping Patel away in its wake. *Here finally,* Patel thought, *is someone who didn't just petition and plead but walked the talk and brought in results.* 'I felt that Gandhi's ten lines had greater force than a hundred-page memorandum,' he would say later when speaking of the impact Gandhi had had on him.

The Swadeshi movement to boycott foreign cloth further strengthened Sardar's resolve. He tossed all his European garments – shirts, coats, gowns, ties, socks and hats – into a huge bonfire in Ahmedabad. From that moment on until the day he died, Patel dressed only in simple khadi clothes woven from the yarn spun by his daughter Mani, adding on a shawl or jacket during the winter.

His transformation surprised his friends. Not only had Patel cast off the foreign clothes that he had loved so much, but he had also taken to living a simple life, eating meals with labourers, sharing their plain food, sleeping on the ground and washing his own clothes. It was almost as if Gandhi had cast a spell on him.

Five years after he had openly mocked Gandhi, Patel became not just his most ardent disciple but also his chief deputy. For the rest of his life, he would address the man whom he had once dismissed as strange, most respectfully as *Bapu*.

> Once upon a time I used to imitate the British and their ways closely. … I used to think then that for our unfortunate country, it was the best policy to imitate the foreigner. I had been taught to think that the people of our country were of poor character and unworthy, and that it was only the foreigner ruling over us who was good and had the ability to improve our condition. We could only be slaves. This was the sort of poison which was being instilled in our minds.

SARDAR PATEL, IN A SPEECH IN 1921

6

UNCHARTED, UNDAUNTED

Hold power accountable

Vallabhbhai returns from England in February 1913, and soon after, he makes a deal with Vithalbhai, his older brother. Vithalbhai would devote his time to the nation, while Vallabhbhai would focus on earning money for the family. This informal agreement does not last long. In 1917, Vallabhbhai too takes a plunge into politics by standing for elections to the Board of the Ahmedabad Municipality, where he becomes chairman of the Sanitary Committee. Soon, he takes on a bold fight against the incompetent commissioner of the municipality and demands his ouster. Nobody has ever attempted to remove a British officer of the Indian Civil Services from his post at the Ahmedabad Municipality before.

'It is shocking.' Patel drew his chair closer to the card table at the Gujarat Club, which he frequented every evening. 'The white residents of the Ahmedabad cantonment receive clean water regularly, but the rest of the city does not.'

'This is precisely why I suggested you join the municipality,' nodded his friend Chimanlal Thakore as he dealt out the deck of shuffled cards. 'We need to have a person like you there to drive positive change.'

'Commissioner Shillidy has got to go…' Patel examined his cards.

'What?' gasped Patel's bridge-playing mates, unprepared to imagine such a dramatic step even though they detested the arrogant commissioner.

'We must demand that he be removed,' insisted Vallabhbhai as he scanned his cards. 'Shillidy ought to be dismissed for incompetence.'

The others at the table exchanged uneasy glances. They all knew Patel was fearless when he appeared in court, never one to tolerate improper behaviour from anyone. Unlike others who were servile and docile, not daring to be discourteous to British officers in positions of power, Vallabhbhai never cowered before authority. Even when a judge appeared to be biased, Patel would openly call it out. Even so, his out-and-out suggestion to have an Englishman removed from office seemed too bold and outrageous.

'How?' Thakore leaned in.

'Do you know about the lake that the municipality filled up to reduce the mosquito menace a few years ago?' Patel reached out for his cigar.

'The one near the railway station?' Thakore cocked his head. 'The one that's being used by Fateh Munshi for his matchstick factory?'

Patel nodded. 'Munshi wants the land. And though he has lost the case multiple times in court and repeated orders have been passed against him to have the land vacated, Shillidy has shielded him, allowing him to use the land because Munshi helped the British during the First World War,' explained Patel. 'Without consulting anybody, Shillidy has recommended that 53,000 square yards of prime land – worth nearly 10 lakh rupees – belonging to the municipality be given to Munshi on a permanent lease.'

'But how does that give you a case to have him removed? He is the commissioner after all...' huffed Thakore disbelievingly. 'A British officer of the Indian Civil Services.'

Not one to fear authority of any kind – white or brown, British or Indian – Patel calmly played his card. 'I've dug into the papers of the case and made a careful study of every detail,' said Patel. 'I have a plan...'

Over the next few days, armed with all the municipal records, Patel prepared to challenge the commissioner. In his arguments, Patel set out how Shillidy had cleverly cut out thirteen key words from the last paragraph of a letter approved by the board before sending it onwards to the government – a clear failure in performing his duty.

Patel's detailed study of the material, coupled with his extraordinary courage, soon bore fruit. A firmly worded resolution was moved against Shillidy, following which he was removed from the post of commissioner. In the years ahead, Patel would go on to become president of the Ahmedabad Municipality and, like several other national leaders, learn the ropes of politics through the management of municipal matters. That incredible political journey began here – by examining facts, by asking questions, by demanding accountability and by taking the powerful to task.

For the first time in history, a British officer of the Indian Civil Services had been removed from his post at the municipality. It filled many with hope that if they had courage, conviction and confidence, Indians could indeed overthrow the British.

> If we are unable to run our village skilfully, honestly and justly, how can we justify our demand for the independence of the country?

STATEMENT IN GANDHI'S SPEECH AT THE GUJARAT POLITICAL CONFERENCE (GODHRA, 1917), WHICH LEFT A LASTING IMPRESSION ON PATEL

7

SAY YES TO THE UNKNOWN

{ Step out of your comfort zone }

In 1917, Kheda district in Gujarat experiences excessive rainfall – over double the annual average, resulting in most sown seeds and crops getting washed away. Soon, an epidemic of plague breaks out, causing further havoc. Kheda is thus experiencing an unusual phenomenon called a green famine *– one caused by too much rain.*

Usually when rains failed, the government gave tax remissions. If the crop was between 25 and 37.5 per cent of the average yield, farmers were allowed to pay half the land revenue a year later. If it was less than 25 per cent, tax collection was postponed. If the crops failed again, the amount was completely remitted. But as a green famine is not perceived to be grave, no relief is forthcoming. Against this background, M.K. Gandhi, who had returned to India from South Africa two years earlier, launches a protest in support of the farmers, the first in which Patel plays a key role.

Patel adjusted his necktie as he listened to Mohanlal Pandya, a farmer leader from Kathalal village, narrating the information he had gathered after surveying villages in Kheda district. It was the eighth day of discussion at Patel's home. It was now time to act.

'I propose that the Gujarat Sabha pass two resolutions,' Patel said thoughtfully. 'First, based on the data collected, we must request the government to postpone the recovery of land revenue. And, second, we should advise the people of Kheda not to pay the tax until a final decision is made.'

Trading his crisp suit and shining shoes for a simple kurta and ordinary chappals, over the next few weeks, Patel camped in an orphanage in Nadiad with Gandhi, who had appealed to the government in letter after letter to postpone the tax on account of crop failure.

Led by Mohanlal Pandya, an application signed by 18,000 farmers was dispatched to the government with an accurate depiction of the problem. But the administration accepted neither Gandhi's arguments nor the farmers' appeals. The sincere appeal having failed, Gandhi then launched what would go down in history as the first attempt in India to defy the authorities by refusing to pay land revenue – the Kheda Satyagraha.

Gandhi asked the farmers of Kheda to take a joint pledge to hold out on paying tax. It would cause them some suffering, he warned them, as government officers were likely to attach their property and take away their cattle to recover the tax due, but truth, he assured them, was on their side.

Over two hundred farmers signed the pledge on the spot, and in a few weeks, more than 3,000 joined in. Always sitting by Gandhi's side, Patel did not speak at the meetings and rallies. Instead, he watched Gandhi closely and dutifully carried out his instructions.

With time, as predicted, the government sent out confiscation notices, imposed fines and took over crops. Milk-giving buffaloes were separated from their calves and kept in the sun to reduce their productivity; threats of arrest were made. When the farmers continued to resist and the revenue could still not be recovered, the government started auctioning people's properties. The battle raged on, with each day bringing on new challenges.

As the weeks wore on, Gandhi was needed elsewhere; he left for Champaran on a tour to Bihar, then to Indore. Having observed Gandhi over months, Patel had learnt from his mentor to observe restraint, to be courteous despite disagreements and to stick strictly to facts during discussions. He was, after all, an experienced barrister, confident of conducting complex trials before demanding magistrates. But could he manage such a large and important public movement?

Overcoming self-doubt, Patel took charge in Gandhi's absence, throwing himself headlong into the struggle. Despite being used to a life of luxury in a city, Patel personally toured hundreds of villages, often on foot in the gruelling heat. He addressed rallies, visited homes and spoke directly to farmers. This was not the path he had chosen for himself; the road was unfamiliar, the destination unclear. But moved by Gandhi's zeal and vision, he persisted. 'The longer the fight lasts, the stiffer is the test which the public will have to pass,' he said, encouraging people to stay strong and stand firm.

Up until that moment, the old guard of the Congress, comprising leaders like Dadabhai Naoroji and Gopal Krishna Gokhale, had believed in the inherent goodness of the British. They had tried persuading them through sincere speeches in closed chambers and wordy appeals in lengthy letters. But Gandhi had given the struggle an entirely new thrust and dimension.

His refreshing approach, which focused on action instead of words, had altered the direction of Patel's life. When the Kheda Satyagraha began, Patel was dressed in a suit and tie. By the time it ended, he was a changed man, leaving locals wondering how their barrister Vallabhbhai, seen until recently in courtrooms in smart European clothes, was now suddenly travelling on bullock carts, dressed in Indian garments. It was not just his outward appearance that underwent a transformation; Kheda triggered a change in behaviour and priorities as well. Fond of cigars, Patel soon gave up smoking. A few years later, he gave up tea. Usually accustomed to eating good-quality rice for both meals, he started eating coarse rice known as *kada*, commonly eaten by farmers. Inspired by Gandhi, he began speaking and writing more often in Gujarati.

On the ground in Kheda, the grit and grind finally bore fruit. Patel's resilience, coupled with the people's resistance, forced the government to back down. The collector issued an order that impoverished farmers were to be let off. The struggle had succeeded – making it the very first time in Indian history that people had fought back against the mighty government by refusing to pay tax and pulled it off through peaceful satyagraha, prompting Patel to remark, 'This fight will act as a spark which will set the whole country afire.'

'This is Vallabhbhai's soil,' Gandhi would later say while speaking about the remarkable transformation the movement had brought about in Patel. 'He has been through the fire…I have no doubt that in the end we shall find pure gold.'

> What I saw of his life then was a revelation to me! He had cast off his foreign dress and along with it the comfortable life he had led before. He lived with the workers, sharing the plain food, sleeping on the ground, doing everything for himself, including the daily washing of his clothes, and walking long distances in villages. … He was his usual self, full of fun and laughter.

ACHARYA KRIPALANI, SPEAKING ABOUT PATEL IN KHEDA

8

SILENT VALOUR

Lead from the front

In 1917, the plague breaks out in Ahmedabad, wiping out 10 per cent of the city's population. Several people, including officials, begin leaving the city. At this time, Vallabhbhai Patel is the chairman of the Sanitary Committee of the Ahmedabad Municipality. Refusing to leave the city for his own personal safety, he stays on, doing his utmost to battle the situation. This is the start of what would become a life spent in public service.

'I am taking my family and leaving for Borsad tomorrow,' the young lawyer said, dabbing his forehead before bundling up his case papers and tossing them over the shelf. 'Nearly everyone I know has gone already. This plague is more lethal than I thought. I don't want to take any chances.' He turned around to the district pleader who was perusing a report at his desk in the court premises. 'Patel Sahib, you too should leave...'

Closing his file, Patel shot the young man a telling glare. 'I am about to leave...' he said, 'to examine the city's sewers.'

The colleague grinned sheepishly and bid farewell as Advocate Patel, who was also then the chairman of the Sanitary Committee of the municipality, turned around and left.

As he picked up pace on his way to Harijan Basti, the young lawyer's words echoed in his ears. The plague was undoubtedly deadly. Thousands had been killed; thousands more were fleeing the city every day. But how could he abandon ship? The words he had heard from Gandhi when he had attended the Gujarat Political Conference rang in his ears: 'In the running of local government lies the key to Swarajya… Unless we improve the condition of our cities, Swarajya will have no meaning for us.'

NO JOB IS TOO MENIAL – PATEL TAKES THE LEAD IN FIGHTING THE PLAGUE

Patel felt the present crisis offered him a snapshot of what Gandhi could have meant. A general did not abandon his fort when it was under attack; instead, he picked up his weapons and walked out to fight. Patel decided to do the same. Starting out in the Dalit quarters of Ahmedabad, he began cleaning the city streets with brooms and dustcarts.

Over the next few weeks, the death toll continued to rise. A great many people migrated out of the city. With the First World War raging in Europe, the demand for goods was soaring, but workers were abandoning their factories and going back to their villages. It was a difficult time.

However, putting his own life at great personal risk, Patel worked round the clock. He personally toured the city, got the sewers cleaned and had the plague-stricken areas disinfected. Watching their leader fulfilling his responsibilities fearlessly out in the field, municipal officials, workers and volunteers were inspired to stay on and follow his lead. He did not order them but simply led by example.

For Patel, this wasn't, after all, his first brush with the virulent disease. He had already dealt with it back in 1901, when he had just moved to Godhra and set up his legal practice there. Nearly every day, news came in that someone had been infected or had died. Then one day, he heard that Ramjibhai, a close friend, was stricken with plague. Aware that he lived alone and had nobody to look after him, Patel had rushed to Ramjibhai's aid and nursed him for days. However, despite his best efforts, Ramjibhai had succumbed to the disease.

While returning after cremating his friend, Patel suspected that he too had been infected with the plague, following which he sent his wife Jhaverben to his parents' home in Karamsad. He then moved to Nadiad and stayed there by himself until he recovered fully.

Even back then, there had been no hope, just death and suffering all around. But he had not lost courage then, and he would not lose it now. Nor would he lose it in the bleak times to follow.

When the plague broke out again between 1932 and 1935 in Borsad district, he would once more be on the ground, touring village after village, setting up relief camps, organizing medical centres, encouraging doctors, consoling patients and devising clever strategies to counter superstitious beliefs people had about the disease. Considering no task too menial, he cleaned houses, swept streets, destroyed dead rats, sprayed antibiotics and burnt sulphur to battle fleas.

Speaking of Patel's extraordinary service during the Ahmedabad plague, his secretary Moolshankar Bhatt later said, 'Immediately after getting the news in the night that plague had broken out in the city, he came out of his house and started helping out people till early in the morning. Municipal workers who came in the morning were astonished to see Patel volunteering for the affected people.'

> One who has taken a pledge to protect the people cannot leave the city even when a single man is there.

PATEL, SPEAKING IN 1942 OF ONE'S DUTIES IN THE CONTEXT OF THE APPROACHING WAR

9

THE CROSSOVER

Actions speak louder than words

It is November 1922; the Kathiawar Political Conference is underway beneath a colourful tent on a large windswept ground. Kathiawar is the peninsular region of Gujarat, which is the home turf of Gandhi, but at this time, Gandhi is in jail in Poona. Patel is not yet a leader of the masses like Gandhi, but he takes upon himself the responsibility to carry on the movement begun by his mentor, calling himself a 'mason' working according to the plan laid down by the 'architect'.*

The conference recommends the abolition of untouchability, an inhuman but common practice in those times, where an entire section of people were regarded as 'impure', and discriminated against. But something ironical is going on at the conference, and it catches Patel's eye.

* *Now Pune*

THE CROSSOVER
KATHIAWAR 1922
I CAN'T BELIEVE THIS!
THAT SIDE! THAT SIDE PLEASE. KEEP SOME DISTANCE. AWAY FROM THE VISITORS ON THIS SIDE!
ARE YOU AWARE THAT THE AGENDA FOR THIS MEETING IS THE ABOLITION OF UNTOUCHABILITY?
RADIO CHICAGO
UH...YES, VALLABHBHAI. WE ARE JUST TRYING TO GET PEOPLE SEATED SO THE MEETING CAN BEGIN.
DO YOU NOT SEE THE IRONY OF THIS? DO I HAVE TO SPELL IT OUT FOR YOU?

AH! THAT! YOU NEEDN'T WORRY, VALLABHBHAI. THE UNTOUCHABLES DON'T HAVE A PROBLEM WITH IT.
DARBAR GOPALDAS-BHAI...YOU ARE THE CHIEF OF CHHAGAM VILLAGE AND PRESIDENT OF THE CONGRESS IN KHEDA DISTRICT...A REFORMED PRINCE WHO HAS ADOPTED GANDHI'S TEACHINGS.
I HAVE COME BECAUSE YOU AND YOUR WIFE BHAKTI-BEN HAVE KINDLY INVITED ME HERE. HOW CAN YOU SIT HERE AND ALLOW THIS TO HAPPEN ?
SIR, I AM THE ORGANIZER... AND I CAN ASSURE YOU THEY ARE COMPLYING WITH THE INSTRUCTIONS WITHOUT ANY PROTEST OR HESITATION.
THESE PEOPLE - MEN, WOMEN, CHILDREN... THEY'VE TRUDGED GREAT DISTANCES, BEARING HOPE IN US TO DELIVER THEM FROM OPPRESSIVE FOREIGN RULE.
BUT WHAT CHANCE DO WE HAVE TO FIGHT AS ONE AGAINST THE MIGHTY BRITISH, WHEN WE CAN'T EVEN SIT TOGETHER AS ONE UNDER A TENT?
CHICAGO

I CANNOT BE A PARTY TO THIS!
VALLABHBHAI... SHU THAYU? THIS IS HOW IT'S ALWAYS BEEN DONE. THE UNTOUCHABLES ARE ALWAYS SEATED IN A SEPARATE ENCLOSURE.
WHAT?
WHY?
VERY WELL, THEN...I SHALL ALSO SIT WITH THEM.
HEY RAM!
NAMASTE, IF YOU DON'T MIND, I AM GOING TO SIT HERE BY YOUR SIDE...
VALLABHBHAI, YOUR PLACE IS ON THE STAGE. PLEASE, PEOPLE HAVE COME TO LISTEN TO YOU SPEAK...

WHEN I AM CALLED UPON TO ADDRESS THE SABHA, I WILL DO SO FROM HERE.'
PATEL SAHIB IS A PATIDAR.
A RESPECTED LAWYER...
THIS IS CONTRARY TO TRADITION...
WHY IS HE SITTING WITH THE UNTOUCHABLES?
AS THE ORGANIZERS FRETTED AND THE CROWDS STARED, PATEL SAT STILL, UNNERVED BY THE SCORNFUL REMARKS ALL AROUND.
HE KNEW THIS WAS THE RIGHT THING TO DO.

I WILL SIT WITH YOU
ME TOO!
WHAT'S WRONG WITH THEM?
BHAKTI-BEN IS THE DAUGHTER OF THE DIWAN OF LIMBDI!
WELCOME... I'M GLAD!
DARBAR GOPALDAS-JI IS A ROYAL! A PRINCE!

WHEN SARDAR FINALLY BEGAN TO SPEAK, HE SPOKE NOT A WORD ABOUT SEGREGATION AND THE INHUMAN PRACTICE HE HAD JUST WITNESSED.
HE DIDN'T NEED TO.
THE CROSSOVER HAD DONE THE TALKING.

> Action appealed to him as nothing else. He believed that a man of words and not of deeds is a garden full of weeds.

MANIBEN PATEL, DAUGHTER OF SARDAR PATEL

STEPPING UP

Gandhiji's arrest in 1922 after a violent incident at Chauri-Chaura and his decision to call off the Non-Cooperation movement came as a blow to many. However, rather than allowing that to derail the momentum, Patel filled the leadership gap and took the reins in his hands, calling it a 'testing time'. 'Now that Gandhiji has gone, what ought his colleagues and disciples to do?' he asked candidly. None among them, Patel said, had the same outstanding character and ability to step into his shoes, and yet he appealed to people to desist from taking all their troubles and worries to Gandhiji for a solution. Stepping up when the need arose, he told people that Mahatma Gandhi had innumerable other problems to solve – 'Let us learn to help ourselves.'

10

MIRROR BEFORE WINDOW

Before judging someone, walk a mile in their shoes

The Swadeshi movement is a key element of India's independence struggle. Begun in 1905 after the partition of Bengal, it acquires new momentum in the 1920s and '30s, after Gandhi calls upon Indians to boycott foreign cloth and spin their own yarn instead. Peaceful picketing is one of the methods used to protest, where groups of volunteers take out processions, urging shopkeepers to stop selling foreign fabric. On 16 October 1922, the Gujarat Provincial Committee decides that shops in Ahmedabad selling foreign cloth should be picketed, and the movement takes off across Gujarat.

Led by Patel and Dr Kanuga, a leading medical practitioner, the large procession made its way down the street towards the bustling bazaar of Ratanpol in Ahmedabad. Some members of the group sang *bhajans* to keep the mood upbeat and non-confrontational, even as others held up placards and echoed slogans to stir people's conscience.

'INQUILAB ZINDABAD!' – the phrase coined by revolutionary poet Maulana Hasrat Mohani, which had become the clarion call of the freedom struggle – resounded down the street.

A year ago, Gandhi had pledged to boycott foreign goods by burning over 1,00,000 garments made of English cloth at the Elphinstone Mill Compound in Bombay. Arguing that India could attain Swaraj or self-rule only if she became self-sufficient, he encouraged people to take up spinning and using homespun khadi garments instead of buying foreign cloth that profited businesses in England. In no time, both khadi and the spinning wheel had emerged as symbols of India's resistance to foreign rule, empowering ordinary people to do their bit in the cause of India's freedom.

'BOYCOTT FOREIGN CLOTH!' Young students raised a cry as they distributed flyers along the route leading to the Ratanpol market, lined with dozens of garment stores. Over the last few weeks, Patel had taken great care to issue pamphlets with detailed instructions to volunteers – they were to give their names and addresses to the police on demand, they were to allow themselves to be arrested if the police so desired, and however violent the police, they were not to retaliate.

Some days ago, Patel himself had tossed all his European clothes – shirts and trousers, ties and hats – garments that he had once much fancied, into a huge bonfire in the city. Moved by Gandhi, Patel's daughter – young Mani – had given it all up, even before her father. Following the beginning in

Ahmedabad, the Swadeshi fire had literally spread to every town and village of Gujarat. Nadiad, Bharuch, Surat – city after city became a fertile ground for picketing. Protesters marched with placards, pasted handbills on walls and lit bonfires to consign foreign garments to flames.

Soon, it came to light that despite the instructions, protesters had turned unruly and used harsh language with the merchants in some places. In some cities, shopkeepers had been coerced into signing pledges, stating that they would not stock foreign cloth for a year. Upon obtaining these pledges by force, the protesters had then ceased their picketing campaigns.

Patel grew annoyed and angry when he heard about these episodes. 'Judging from what I have learnt...I can assure you that the various epithets we have been using for the merchants – scoundrels, dishonest fellows, thieves – are all epithets that could more appropriately be applied to us rather than to them,' he thundered.

Getting pledges under duress, in Patel's view, was just not the right approach. If the boycott was to have any impact at all, the change had to come from within; merchants had to be persuaded to stop selling foreign cloth of their own volition. Besides, the onus was as much on the people to not buy or use foreign cloth as it was on the merchants to not sell it. Simply transferring the burden on to someone else was rather convenient and completely pointless.

'We did not have any business commitments,' Patel argued, urging the picketers to show empathy and step into the merchants' shoes for a moment. 'All we had to do was to set fire to the foreign cloth we might have in our houses, worth a hundred or two hundred rupees. We had, at the most, to withdraw from government schools one or two of our boys. … For the merchants, on the other hand, it is a question of giving up their sole or main source of livelihood.'

Urging the protesters to act with respect, he made it clear that the use of foul language or any kind of threat or force was simply unacceptable. Cautioning them about their needlessly judgemental manner, he said, 'We do not examine our own actions and are only too anxious to ask others to render account. It is our duty today to encourage the merchants in the good start they have made and not to say anything which would render their task more difficult and make them despair. If during this intervening period we all change over to the use of Indian cloth, why would they want to import any more foreign cloth?'

"We seem to devote too much time to things that hardly matter, and too little to those that count. We talk, while the paramount need is that of action. We are critical of other people's exertions but lack the will to contribute our own. We are trying to overtake others by giant strides while we have hardly learnt to walk."

SARDAR PATEL, IN HIS ADDRESS TO THE NATION ON 15 AUGUST 1950

11

STORMS PASS, BONDS STAY

Balance your boundaries

It is 1922. A group of Congress members, such as party president Chittaranjan Das and senior leader Motilal Nehru, suggest a change in approach. They argue that adopting spinning and attacking untouchability are unlikely to win India independence. They suggest, instead, that leaders stand for elections to the legislative councils. Vithalbhai Patel (Sardar's older brother) is a vocal supporter of this group, called the 'Pro-Changers'. Vallabhbhai Patel, on the other hand, is firmly opposed to this idea and is in the camp known as 'No-Changers'. As the clash between the two groups intensifies, both brothers find themselves on opposite sides of a widening political divide.

'Let us use the councils against the Raj,' Congress President Chittaranjan Das thundered into the microphone at the annual session of the party in Gaya. 'Until now we have boycotted them and held that those sitting in the legislature are not the true representatives of the people of India. But I think it is our duty to go inside the legislature and carry out a more effective boycott.'

'Let's wreck the councils' was a slogan heard among the crowds gathered in the huge tent.

'The idea of boycotting implies something more than merely keeping away,' Das continued. 'If an army enters enemy territory, it does not mean the army is cooperating with the enemy. In the same way, if we enter the legislature, we are not cooperating. It all comes down to the goal with which we are entering.'

The slogan 'Wreck the councils' caught on.

'I disagree,' Congress leader C. Rajagopalachari from Madras,* affectionately called Rajaji, stood up to speak. 'I oppose council entry...it will do us positive harm. If the Congress agrees to participate in the legislature, it will mean an end to non-cooperation. This will distract us and spoil all that we have achieved so far.'

'I agree.' Rajendra Prasad, a Congress leader from the United Provinces, raised his hand. 'I also oppose entry into the legislature.'

'Me too...' added Congressman Dr Mukhtar Ahmad Ansari.

'I am also in agreement with Rajaji,' said Vallabhbhai Patel. 'I am not a leader; I am a soldier...the son of a peasant. I do not believe we can gain Independence by merely talking. We shall not be able to fight the government on its own ground.' Patel explained, 'Once we enter the legislature,

**Now Chennai*

people will lose their enthusiasm for Independence and the Congress will lose the confidence of the people. Even if we conduct a campaign for a hundred years through the legislature, we will not get Independence.'

After both sides had discussed and debated the issue, it was put to vote. Rajaji and his group advocating a complete boycott won the contest.

Disillusioned with the result, Congress President Das resigned from his post and broke off into a new party called the Swaraj Party. Motilal Nehru, Hakim Ajmal Khan and Vithalbhai Patel joined him. Consequently, the Congress party was split down its middle, with one group supporting constructive work among the masses and boycotting the council, called the 'No-changers', and the other group supporting entry into the legislature, called the 'Pro-changers' or the Swarajists.

'Why don't you understand?' Vithalbhai argued with his younger brother once he got back home. 'Entry into the legislature is like smuggling into the enemy fort to conquer it. We aren't going in to cooperate with the enemy.'

'The fortress of the enemy is not located in the legislature,' retorted Vallabhbhai, trying to reason with his brother. 'This government will continue to function even for a hundred years without a legislature. Their true power lies elsewhere. Governors and viceroys can rule through other methods regardless of what the councils say or do.'

Over the next few weeks, both brothers tried persuading each other, but neither managed to change the other's mind. Despite ties of blood, both brothers were clearly opposed to the other's views.

Soon, Vithalbhai's manner with his younger brother began to change. He was often stern and seldom polite. 'There is no reply to my letter,' he would pull up Vallabhbhai when he was a member of the legislature. 'What is the reason? I will be living in Delhi from 1 December, and everything should be ready when I get there.'

Despite Vallabhbhai's rising stature in the Congress and the country, he never showed disrespect, only restraint. Even though Vithalbhai is said to have often poked fun at his younger brother, calling him all kinds of names to the amusement of his friends, Vallabhbhai refused to be provoked by his brother's remarks.

Ultimately, the brothers entered into another pact. Some years ago, they had decided that Vithalbhai would devote himself to the nation while Vallabhbhai would focus on earning for the family. That understanding had not lasted long, with Vallabhbhai also taking to politics. But this new one lasted till death tore them apart. Agreeing not to clash before the public and embitter relations, they mutually decided that Vithalbhai would not campaign in Ahmedabad, and Vallabhbhai would not carry out any propaganda in Bombay.

However, when Vithalbhai visited Ahmedabad, he stayed with Vallabhbhai, who would kneel by his side and remove his older brother's shoes when he arrived, always treating him with the utmost respect. Later, when he left to return, Vallabhbhai would slip money into his brother's coat and never breathe a word about it. The differences between them, which led to many a heated political debate, did little to sour their personal relationship.

> We have to make sure that there is no disparity between the language of the heart and the language of the lips.

SARDAR PATEL, IN A SPEECH HE DELIVERED IN HYDERABAD IN 1949

12

QUICK ON THE COMEBACK

Harness the power of wit

Nearly everyone who interacts with Patel is bowled over by his wit. From pulling out suitable proverbs in Gujarati for the occasion to responding to challenging questions with wry humour, Patel's wisecracks and quips cut a sharp contrast to his otherwise sombre and senatorial appearance. Sardar is at his wittiest best when confronted with seemingly pointless questions or what he sees as infuriating practices.

In 1923, Patel was elected as the president of a political conference in Maharashtra. This was the stage of the freedom movement when the Swadeshi ideology was at its height. Thousands, like Sardar himself, were throwing their foreign garments into bonfires and beginning to adopt clothes made from homespun khadi.

'I would like to ask a question.' A person raised his hand at the meeting. 'I wish to know if it is alright if one wears a homespun khadi coat but a dhoti spun in a mill?'

Smiling slightly at the schoolchild-like question, Sardar leaned towards the microphone. 'Such persons shall be allowed to cast only half a vote!'

He replied in a similar vein when someone once asked Gandhi, 'Bapu, how can we avoid trampling upon ants when we walk so that we may practise non-violence?'

'Tell him,' Patel nudged Gandhi, 'to walk with his feet on his head!'

A man once wrote to Gandhi asking for advice. He said he did not like his wife because she was ugly and asked for Gandhi's opinion on what he should do. 'Tell him,' said Patel to Gandhi, 'to solve this problem by taking his eyes out. Then he won't have to suffer her ugliness.'

Most people treated Gandhi with reverence, as did Patel. But Vallabhbhai was one of the few who pulled Gandhi's leg and joked with him as a friend. Once, wanting to use both hands dexterously, Gandhi began an experiment to spin the *charkha* with his left hand. 'You're going to waste more cotton than you spin,' Patel said, trying to discourage Gandhi's new fad. But when Gandhi was not dissuaded, knowing how people were wont to follow anything Gandhi did, Patel remarked, 'Now for heaven's sake, don't broadcast this, otherwise the whole ashram will start spinning with the left hand.'

When they were in jail together, Patel would often prepare Gandhi's morning drink by adding honey, baking soda and fresh lime in warm water. Once, lemons were not available, and Gandhi suggested that Patel use tamarind as a souring agent since there were many tamarind trees on the jail premises.

'Bapu, surely you know that tamarind causes rheumatism and weakens the bones,' said Patel.

'Is that so?' asked Gandhi earnestly. 'But Jamnalal Bajaj seems to be having it, and he has no problem.'

'He may be…' laughed Patel, imagining the plump Mr Bajaj, 'but in his case, the tamarind cannot reach his bones.'

One day, again in Yerwada Jail, in 1932, Gandhi received a letter from an irate correspondent signed as 'one who has the misfortune of living in your age'.

'What sort of reply should I send him?' Gandhi asked Vallabhbhai.

'Tell him to poison himself,' replied Patel casually.

'Would it not be better to say that he should poison me?' asked Gandhi cheekily.

'I'm afraid that will not help him,' replied Patel matter-of-factly. 'If he poisons you and you die, he will be sentenced to death. Then he would take rebirth along with you. It is much better that he poisons himself.'

Even as his body aged, Sardar continued his quick-witted repartee. In July 1949, a leading socialist named Asoka Mehta criticized Sardar's economic policies, claiming rich capitalists were leading Patel down the wrong track.

Sardar had little patience for socialists, who he thought wasted much time discussing ideological theories and delivering lofty speeches instead of doing constructive

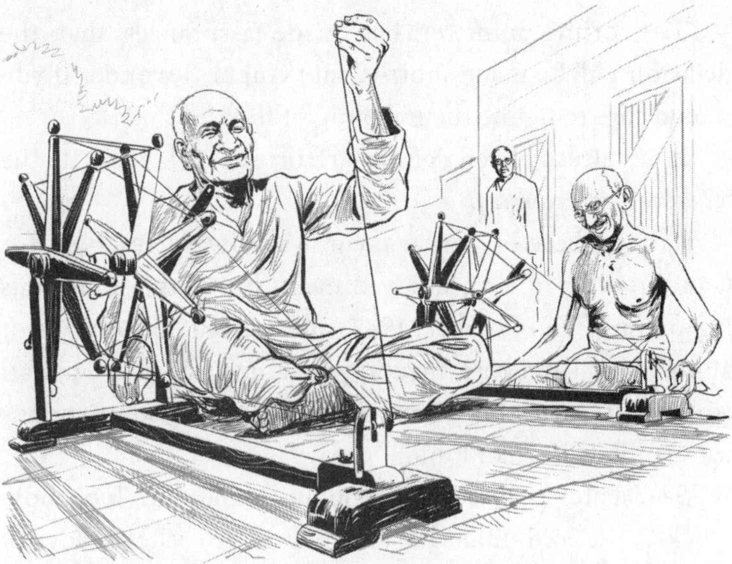

VALLABHBHAI IS ONE OF THE FEW LEADERS WHO PLAYFULLY TEASE GANDHI AND PULL HIS LEG

work. Responding to one such attack about inequality in the country, and in particular, about the wealth of a specific industrialist, Sardar said, 'I know how much money he has... if all his wealth were to be divided equally among all Indians, your share will come to about four annas...I will give it to you from my own pocket if you agree to stop talking...'

Patel usually spoke little. He was often seen sitting at meetings with his eyes half closed, almost as if he were dozing off. But when he rose to speak, it is said the benches filled up with people eager to listen. In February 1948, a question was put to Patel by Congress leader Deshbandhu Gupta about a certain matter under discussion in Parliament.

'The prime minister has made assurances that the decision will be made shortly,' said Gupta. 'I wonder if you would care to define the meaning of *shortly*.'

'It has already been defined,' retorted Patel. 'Look up the Webster's dictionary.'

But the best of Sardar's wit was always reserved for Gandhi, who in turn enjoyed every bit of the humorous leg-pulling. In October 1947, an unwell Gandhi went along with Patel to a meeting organized by the Gujarati community in Delhi, who wished to donate some money for Gandhi's Harijan Fund.

'See,' Patel pointed to a coughing Gandhi, 'look how quickly the old man has recovered to relieve you of your money!'

> Sardar will not miss a laugh even at the foot of the gallows!

GANDHI, SPEAKING ABOUT PATEL IN OCTOBER 1947

13

GOING THE WHOLE HOG

Fight it out, then move on

During 1922–23, dacoity has become rampant in the Borsad taluka *of Gujarat. The police accuse the locals of colluding with the dacoits and aiding them. Meanwhile, the local people deny the charge and claim instead that the police are helping the dacoits get away.*

Agreeing with the police, the government imposes a special punitive tax on the people of Borsad in order to cover the cost of increased policing to deal with the rising numbers of robberies and murders. This special tax is called The Outlaws and Punitive Police Tax, under which a tax of 2,40,074 rupees is imposed on the taluka, *and it is to be recovered from all the residents above the age of 16 to cover the cost of increased policing. The locals complain that this is an unjust measure and take the matter to Vallabhbhai.*

GOING THE WHOLE HOG
BORSAD 1922-23
THESE RECORDS SUGGEST THAT DACOITY CASES IN YOUR DISTRICT HAVE SEEN AN ALARMING INCREASE RECENTLY...
YES, THAT IS SO.
THE GOVERNMENT WANTS US TO PAY FOR THE ADDITIONAL POLICE TO NAB THE DACOITS. BUT WE ARE NOT TO BLAME FOR THE DACOITY. WHY MUST WE BEAR THIS TAX?
THE POLICE BLAME US, SAYING WE ARE SHELTERING THE DACOITS. THAT IS SIMPLY NOT TRUE. IT IS THE POLICE WHO ARE WORKING IN COLLUSION WITH THE DACOITS.
ON WHAT BASIS DO YOU SAY SO?
THE ROBBERIES ARE TAKING PLACE WITH FULL KNOWLEDGE OF THE POLICE. MANY PEOPLE WHO'VE SUPPLIED INFORMATION TO THE POLICE ABOUT THE DACOITS HAVE HAD TO PAY FOR IT WITH THEIR LIVES.

PATEL LISTENED CAREFULLY AS LOCAL LEADER MOHANLAL PANDYA AND SOCIAL WORKER RAVISHANKAR MAHARAJ NARRATED HOW THE POLICE HAD DELIBERATELY FAILED TO ARREST THE DACOITS.
THEN, HE STUDIED THE ORDER OF SEPTEMBER 1923 WHICH IMPOSED A PUNITIVE TAX OF OVER TWO LAKH RUPEES ON THE PEOPLE OF BORSAD, TO BE RECOVERED FROM EVERY RESIDENT OVER SIXTEEN YEARS OF AGE.
I WOULD LIKE YOU BOTH TO GO TO BORSAD. GATHER INFORMATION FROM EVERY VILLAGE ABOUT WHAT EXACTLY HAPPENED THERE. COME BACK WITH A FULL REPORT.
OVER THE NEXT FEW WEEKS, PANDYA AND MAHARAJ TOURED VILLAGE AFTER VILLAGE IN BORSAD, GATHERING EVIDENCE, SPEAKING TO RESIDENTS AND NOTING DOWN DETAILS.
BABAR DEVA IS A DANGEROUS DACOIT OPERATING IN THIS REGION. HE HAS A BIG GANG.
THEY RETURNED TO PATEL ARMED WITH ALL THE NECESSARY INFORMATION.

THERE'S ANOTHER DACOIT NAMED ALI. HE ALSO HAS A GANG.
BOTH GANGS OPERATE ON HORSEBACK AND CARRY GUNS. THEY'VE WRECKED OUR LIVES.'
SARDAR TURNED THE PAGES OF THE DETAILED ENQUIRY PANDYA AND MAHARAJ HAD CONDUCTED, AS HE LISTENED TO THEIR REPORT.
BOTH DACOITS HAVE COMMITTED SEVERAL ROBBERIES. IF BABAR DEVA SUSPECTS SOMEONE IS GIVING INFORMATION ABOUT HIM TO THE POLICE, HE KILLS THEM.
HE DIDN'T EVEN SPARE HIS OWN MOTHER, WIFE AND RELATIVES. HE IS RUTHLESS.

OUR INVESTIGATION FOUND THAT IN SEVERAL INSTANCES, EVEN WHEN THE POLICE HAD A CHANCE TO ARREST HIM, THEY DID NOT.
REPORT
BORSAD
THERE IS NO DOUBT THAT THE POLICE ARE IN CAHOOTS WITH THE BANDITS. THE PEOPLE ARE VICTIMS, NOT COLLABORATORS. THEY SHOULD NOT BE MADE TO BEAR THIS UNJUST TAX.
HMM... IT SEEMS CLEAR FROM YOUR STUDY REPORT THAT THE PEOPLE OR BORSAD ARE SUFFERING ON TWO FRONTS. THEY'RE LIVING IN FEAR OF THE DACOITS. AND THEY'RE BEING WRONGLY ACCUSED OF AIDING THE DACOITS.
IF THE POLICE ARE ACTING DISHONESTLY AND THE PUNITIVE TAX IS INDEED UNJUST, WE HAVE TO EXPOSE THIS UGLY NEXUS.
WHY SHOULD THE GOVERNMENT MALIGN OUR NAME? THE FIGHT IS NOT ABOUT MONEY. IT IS A FIGHT ABOUT SELF-WORTH.

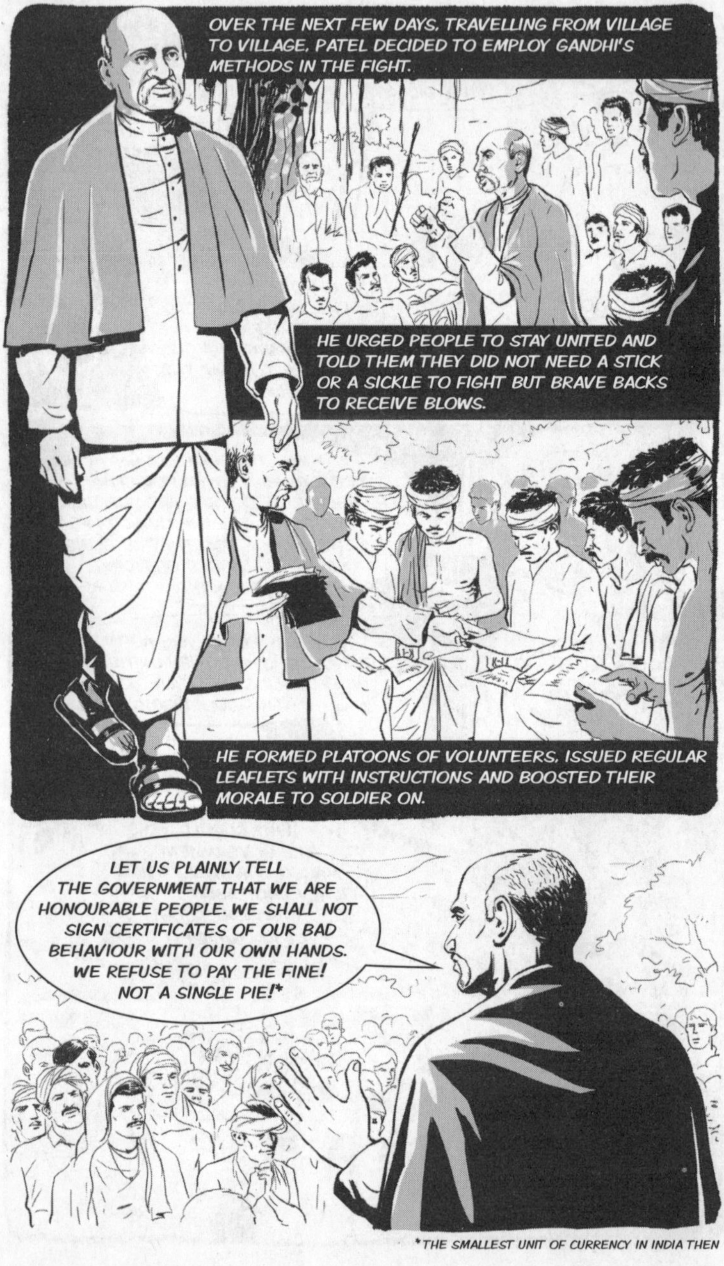

*THE SMALLEST UNIT OF CURRENCY IN INDIA THEN

BASED ON HIS EXTENSIVE HOMEWORK, PATEL ALSO FILED A DETAILED REPORT WITH THE GOVERNMENT ENUMERATING MANY INSTANCES IN BANJEDA, BEDWA, SUNAV AND SEVERAL OTHER VILLAGES, WHERE PEOPLE HAD SUFFERED FOR HELPING THE POLICE.
A MAN NAMED BAKORE WHO HAD HELPED THE POLICE HAD BEEN SHOT BY BABAR DEVA.
A POTTER IN BORSAD HAD BEEN STABBED IN THE CHEST BY THE BANDIT.
A TAILOR HAD BEEN BADLY ATTACKED AFTER HE'D PROVIDED INFORMATION ABOUT THE DACOITS.
BABAR DEVA MURDERED 22 PEOPLE BECAUSE THEY INFORMED THE POLICE ABOUT HIS WHEREABOUTS. BUT THE GOVERNMENT STILL ARGUES THAT PEOPLE DID NOT GIVE INFORMATION! MAY I ASK HOW MANY POLICEMEN WERE MURDERED IN THIS CHASE?
ANGERED BY THE MOVEMENT AND PATEL'S ARGUMENTS, THE POLICE AND GOVERNMENT OFFICIALS RESISTED.
CONFISCATE THEIR PROPERTY! TAKE AWAY THEIR CATTLE! WE SHALL RECOVER THE DACOITY TAX FROM THE PEOPLE OF BORSAD ONE WAY OR THE OTHER!
DO NOT BE AFRAID OF THE GOVERNMENT. UNDER NO CIRCUMSTANCES SHOULD YOU PAY OR REACT VIOLENTLY. TRUTH IS ON YOUR SIDE!

AS A LAWYER, PATEL KNEW THAT, UNDER THE LAW, OFFICIALS COULD NOT ATTACH PROPERTIES AFTER SUNSET. SO HE DEVISED A CLEVER GAME PLAN.
WHEN A GOVERNMENT OFFICIAL WAS SEEN APPROACHING A VILLAGE TO ATTACH HOMES OR CATTLE TO RECOVER THE UNPAID TAX, A VOLUNTEER WAITING ATOP A TREE WOULD BEAT A DRUM.
THE VILLAGERS WOULD IMMEDIATELY LOCK THEIR HOUSES, TAKE THEIR CATTLE OUT FOR GRAZING AND LEAVE THE VILLAGE FOR THE DAY.
VILLAGE AFTER VILLAGE WAS FOUND EMPTY AND DESOLATE WHEN THE ATTACHMENT OFFICERS VISITED.
THE VILLAGES WOULD RETURN TO NORMAL AT NIGHT WHEN RESIDENTS RETURNED AFTER THE OFFICERS HAD LEFT EMPTY-HANDED.
SECRET & CONFIDENTIAL
IT WAS A NOVEL STYLE OF BOYCOTT. BUT PATEL ALSO KEPT UP WITH HIS METICULOUS RESEARCH.

IN THE PROCESS, HE DISCOVERED A SECRET CIRCULAR OF THE DISTRICT SUPERINTENDENT OF POLICE THAT INSTRUCTED SUB-INSPECTORS TO TURN A BLIND EYE TO DACOITIES COMMITTED BY ALI, AS HE HAD PROMISED TO ASSIST IN THE ARREST OF BABAR DEVA. PATEL DECIDED TO EXPOSE THE GOVERNMENT.
IN ORDER TO ARREST ONE DACOIT, GOVERNMENT OFFICERS THOUGHT IT WISE TO SEEK THE ASSISTANCE OF ANOTHER OUTLAW!
THE GOVERNMENT FURNISHED ALI WITH ARMS AND AMMUNITION AND ALLOWED HIM TO COMMIT DACOITIES AND MURDERS AT WILL. THE GOVERNMENT HAS BETRAYED THE PEOPLE!
FACED WITH SUCH FORMIDABLE EVIDENCE, GOVERNOR OF BOMBAY LESLIE WILSON ORDERED AN IMMEDIATE INVESTIGATION INTO THE MATTER.
TO ENSURE THAT THE ENQUIRY IS CONDUCTED IMPARTIALLY, I SHALL NOT PARTICIPATE IN IT. LET THE PEOPLE OF BORSAD MAKE THEIR OWN CASE.
THE GOVERNMENT HAS DECIDED TO WITHDRAW THE PUNITIVE DACOITY TAX IN BORSAD. THE COST OF THE EXTRA POLICING WILL BE COVERED FROM THE GENERAL REVENUES OF THE GOVERNMENT.

IT WAS A THRILLING VICTORY FOR THE PEOPLE OF BORSAD.
JUSTICE!
VICTORY!
WE WON !!
VICTORY!
YOU HAVE NOT SUCCEEDED BECAUSE OF MY SKILL OR CLEVERNESS. TODAY WE HAVE GAINED THIS VICTORY BECAUSE WE WALKED ALONG THE ROAD SHOWN BY GANDHIJI. BUT OUR MAIN BIG QUARREL...INDEPENDENCE... IS STILL UNRESOLVED.
BUT EVEN AS PEOPLE CELEBRATED, PATEL WAS QUICK TO WARN THEM NOT TO BE ANGRY WITH THE POLICEMEN AND OFFICIALS OVER THEIR UNJUST ACTIONS.
LET GOODWILL AND FRIENDSHIP REIGN HEREAFTER. LET THERE BE NO HARASSMENT OR PUNISHMENT OF OFFICIALS WHO CARRIED OUT THEIR DUTIES OR THOSE WHO PAID UP THE TAX.
AS FAR AS PATEL WAS CONCERNED, THE PRESENT BATTLE WAS OVER. IT WAS TIME TO MOVE ON.

> During this short struggle, consider what great sacrifices you have made, what courage you have exhibited, what unity you have maintained and what enthusiasm you have shown. It is only because you have shown yourself capable of these that you have been able to obtain what you wanted.

SARDAR PATEL

STEPPING UP

After India became independent, when Patel was the home minister, he once asked Home Secretary H.V. Iengar what he thought of a senior Congress leader. 'Sir, you know him a great deal better than me,' replied Iengar, taken aback that Patel should ask for his opinion about the man.

'I may have known him for long,' replied Patel, 'but how do I know that my impression is not prejudiced? Between my own knowledge and what you are able to tell me, I may be able to get a more balanced picture.'

Thorough groundwork, which involved examining an issue from all perspectives, and meticulous homework always preceded Patel's actions, whether it was in his capacity as a lawyer, an activist or later on as a minister.

14

NO OFFENCE

{ You can be assertive without being aggressive }

In April 1923, it is decided to hold a peaceful flag procession in Nagpur, the capital of the Central Provinces. However, as volunteers march through Nagpur's Civil Lines area with the Swaraj flag, they are beaten and flung into drains by the police. Despite the backlash, the Nagpur District Congress Committee decides to go on with the plan. From May to August, volunteers walk with the flag every single day, and each day, more and more people are arrested. As the struggle intensifies, Vallabhbhai Patel is called upon to take command of the Nagpur Flag Satyagraha.

'This is a shame!' Patel examined the sheet enlisting the charges against those arrested that week. 'People are being detained on the flimsiest of grounds.'

'Patel Sahib,' said a local Congress worker, 'Mr Clarke, the commissioner of Nagpur, lives in Civil Lines. And he is adamant that the flag must not be carried past his house.'

'He has even declared,' said another, 'that if he finds a flag-bearer marching in front of his bungalow, he would shoot at them.'

'Hmm...' Patel nodded, holding up the newspaper. Not only was Clarke the commissioner of Nagpur, but he was also the secretary of the Association of Officers of the Indian Civil Services, not to mention a correspondent for influential newspapers. The Flag Satyagraha, Clarke had written in *The Times of India*, was aimed at harassing Europeans living in the Civil Lines. 'This is such false propaganda...our intention is not to trouble anybody, only to carry our flag,' said Patel, conscious that they were dealing with a clever and powerful opponent.

'Over 1,000 people have already been arrested,' another volunteer shook his head despondently. 'A venerable social reformer like Acharya Vinoba Bhave is being made to crush stones under the hot sun in Akola Jail. Ravishankar Maharaj is in a cell in Nagpur, grinding 25 kilos of grain on the *chakki* daily. Prisoners who don't finish their tasks are being put in solitary confinement.'

'And, sir...the food in the jail is appalling,' intervened another who had just visited the inmates. 'The dal has more dirt than pulses. The rotis are full of pebbles. Prisoners are being hustled through doorless latrines.'

Sitting back with his eyes closed, Patel took stock of the situation. While it was nobody's intention to humiliate Europeans, it was being projected in that manner by the crafty commissioner. But that was not the issue in question at all. It was only a matter of asserting the right to carry the flag in public. Patel was clear they couldn't concede ground on this one.

'Regardless,' nodded industrialist Jamnalal Bajaj, friend and ardent supporter of Gandhi, 'we must not back down. Let us fight on. I shall take the lead in the procession tomorrow.'

'Absolutely,' agreed Patel, charged by the challenge this movement posed. 'It's a beautiful fight. It must go on.'

Taking control of the satyagraha, Patel asked for fifty candidates to volunteer for prison each day. And he got nearly what he wanted. Each day, groups of people walked with the flag through Civil Lines, and each day the police arrested them.

As weeks passed, Patel called for volunteers from Gujarat; Rajaji sent groups from Madras; another contingent arrived from Mysore. Apart from organizing the daily march, Patel also put his craft of negotiation to work by reaching out to his brother Vithalbhai, who knew the governor of the Central Provinces, Sir Frank Sly.

'Europeans are not the target of our satyagraha at all,' Patel said repeatedly, clarifying the stance. It was only about asserting the right of Indians to carry their flag in peaceful public processions. He instructed his people that nobody was to raise a slogan while passing a church; nobody was to raise a slogan while passing the houses of Europeans. They were to strictly observe silence. And upon reaching Sadar Bazaar, they were to disperse peacefully. The intent was made clear time and again: The goal was not to harass or humiliate anybody but to claim one's dignity and express one's identity.

The overcrowded prisons coupled with Patel's tactful negotiations finally forced the government to relent. It was announced that a group of hundred people would be permitted to carry the flag through Civil Lines at noon on 18 August 1923, and all prisoners held so far for the Flag Satyagraha would be released.

For the very first time, Vallabhbhai Patel of Gujarat had been called upon to take charge of a movement outside his home turf in the role of commander. And it had ended in vindication and victory.

> Patel's valour was as high as the mountains; his determination, as strong as steel.

MAULANA AZAD, CONGRESS LEADER AND POST-INDEPENDENCE MINISTER OF EDUCATION

15

REALITY CHECK

Test the waters before jumping in

In 1920–21, Gandhi launched the Non-Cooperation Movement, which helped turn the struggle for independence into a nationwide mass movement. Many events were held all over the country. Gandhi was invited to tour Kutch in 1925 to foster the movement there. Patel and some others accompanied him on the tour.*

Pleased to see the crowd that had turned up to receive him at Mandvi port, Gandhi folded his hands to greet them as he stepped out of the steamer. 'People are coming out in large numbers to support the struggle,' he noted with satisfaction, as those present showered him with garlands. 'If our people stand united like this, nothing can stop us from throwing off British rule.'

A step behind Gandhi, Patel surveyed the crowds thronging for a glimpse of Bapu. Impulsively, he decided to try a bold experiment.

* *Now Kachchh*

As they made their way out of the port, Patel leaned in to speak to the man who had invited Gandhi to Kutch and was going to be their host tonight. 'Have you met our friend there?' He pointed to Gandhi's new private secretary walking a few steps ahead of him. 'His name is Krishnadas, and he is a Harijan.'

'I see...' the host nodded. 'I'm curious to know who that little girl walking beside Bapu is...'

'Ah...that little girl...' Patel smiled. 'Do you know Dudhabhai...the Harijan at Gandhi's ashram? She is his daughter, Lakshmi. Bapu has adopted her as his own daughter.'

'An untouchable?' asked a man walking behind Patel.

'That's right...' Patel nodded earnestly, although the girl by Gandhi's side was not really Lakshmi. 'You see...Bapu really means what he says. He walks the talk.'

'We have no problem at all...' said the host. 'We do not believe in untouchability.'

'That's wonderful,' said Patel, noticing a change in the expressions of some others around him. 'I am glad to know that. You better attend to Krishnadas and Lakshmi with care, because they are very special to Gandhi.'

'Did you hear that?' A turbaned man walking behind Patel gasped. 'Bapu has brought along untouchables. That girl is an *antyaja* (untouchable).'

'I heard he does that. My cousin in Kothara village warned me about it. I don't know why he would defile us all with their presence like this.'

Alert to the whispers and stares all around him, Patel walked on, a smug smile pinned upon his face. If Gandhi believed that Indians had united as one, perhaps this would give him a dose of reality.

Once inside the home of their host for the night, Patel told other members of their group about his little game and asked them all to play along.

'You are a cheeky fellow,' Gandhi admonished Patel.

'A prank in good spirit…' chuckled Patel. 'Let's see what comes of it.'

As it turned out, the prank would do more to reveal the true picture than any study report ever could.

'That child with Bapu…' The news spread like wildfire among the people of Mandvi and others along the route who had invited Gandhi. 'She is his adopted Harijan daughter…'

'That man Krishnadas is a Harijan too…and they are both staying with Bapu.'

People turned their faces away. Some of them decided to keep their distance.

'How can we take them into our house?'

'Impossible! They will pollute our homes.'

'Why did Bapu have to bring along these people?'

Very soon, that's all many were talking about.

'I'm so sorry…' a chieftain who had invited Gandhi to his village apologized to Patel. 'Now that our people know there are two *antyaja*s in your group, they are not willing to receive Gandhi into their homes.'

'But Bapu is very particular about keeping to the schedule,' said Patel, throwing Gandhi an all-knowing glance as he wondered if this was to be the fate of most of their Kutch tour. 'He will not change the programme.'

'I'm sorry, but people are not willing to invite you into their homes if you are going to bring two untouchables along. At best, I can arrange for the group to stay at the public rest house...'

At one meeting, the chairman sat some feet away from Gandhi, and after reading the welcome address, he threw it into Gandhi's hands, unwilling to touch him since Gandhi had lived among untouchables.

Elsewhere, the entourage was served food in leaf-dishes and not in the brass vessels that were usually used.

In some villages, people entertained Gandhi's group, but afterwards, they washed out their homes.

In some cases, rotis were thrown into their plates from a distance, as people feared being polluted by their touch.

In yet another village, simply nobody agreed to cook a meal for Gandhi and his group.

Often, those who had agreed to host Gandhi declined to do so.

In several places, the meetings and rallies he addressed were disturbed by those who did not want untouchables in their midst.

Despite the inconveniences, Patel continued with the ruse throughout the tour so that Gandhi could have a true picture of what he was up against. Pranks could be mischievous. But sometimes, they were most helpful in revealing hard truths.

Patel was, after all, a son of the soil and knew how rigorously caste taboos were observed in the countryside.

He wanted to help Gandhi see through the smokescreen, and if a prank could help open one's eyes to reality, then it was well worth the while.

> It will be folly to ignore realities; facts take their revenge if they are not faced squarely and well.

SARDAR PATEL, AS QUOTED BY V.P. MENON, IN *INTEGRATION OF THE INDIAN STATES*

16

LOVE OVER EGO

Don't cash in on grief

In 1927, Patel is the president of the Ahmedabad Municipality. On the weekend of 23 July, unusually heavy rains lash the city, and the downpour continues with fury into the night. Unable to sit in the comfort of his home when the city is drowning, Patel sets off in the middle of the wet and windy night to personally inspect the city and fix the damage. Not one to sit complacently and gloat over fulfilling his responsibilities in the city, Patel then goes the extra mile to extend help to those suffering the downpour outside city limits.

'Vallabhbhai?' Harilal Kapadia held up the hurricane lamp in his hand, shocked to see his drenched friend at the door. He turned to the clock behind him. It was well past midnight. 'What are you doing out on such a night?'

'Come with me!' shouted Patel, his voice partly swallowed by the gusting wind and rain. 'The situation is grim. We need to inspect how the city is holding up.'

'In this blessed rain?' Kapadia looked mortified. He had been worried sick, wondering which of his walls was going to collapse after the beating they had received from the whipping wind, and here Patel wanted to take a tour of the city. 'Now?' he asked.

'We need to swing into action,' said Patel sombrely. 'There isn't a minute to be wasted.'

'Let me offer you a cup of hot tea first,' said Kapadia, feeling sorry for the dripping figure at the door. 'And a change of clothes.'

Before long, Patel and Kapadia were wading through knee-deep water, walking to the home of the municipal engineer, Gore.

Awoken from his sleep, Gore was taken to the municipal office. Urgent messages were sent out to all concerned staff, summoning them immediately to work.

'During my inspection, I noticed these broken culverts,' Patel pointed out to the staff that had been hurriedly summoned in the dead of the night. 'Major drains here, here and here need to be repaired...'

Under Patel's supervision, before the next morning's sunrise, arrangements had been put in place to drain the floodwaters in low-lying areas.

Yet, there was still much to do. Thousands of homes had collapsed in the city, and tens of thousands of people had been rendered homeless. Moreover, the rains had not stopped yet, leading to growing concern about people outside the city.

Deciding to act, Patel drew up a list of courageous and capable people to take command – Lakshmidas Asher, Narhari Parikh, Maganlal Gandhi, Dr Chandulal, Kishorlal Mashruwala and Amritlal Thakkar, among others. He appointed them to take charge of relief efforts in Nadiad, Anand, Mahemdabad, Broach and Baroda,* instructing them to ensure that help reached every village under their charge.

He knew it wasn't easy to get anywhere; it had taken him nearly three days to reach Sabarmati Ashram within Ahmedabad city itself. Trains had stopped running, postal traffic had come to a standstill and the telegraph service was severely disrupted. Getting news from or getting relief to any place had become virtually impossible.

Putting their own lives at risk, Patel and his team travelled somehow to the remotest of villages. Sometimes, they walked for hours through waist-deep water and mud. At other times, they swam across rivers with the help of inflated bags.

Soon, detailed reports of the damage began to trickle in. In village after village, people had lost everything – their homes, their cattle, their goods. Low-lying areas were completely submerged, and people had moved to higher ground. When the waters rose higher, people climbed onto trees, clinging to the branches for dear life.

It came to light that in a village near the River Dhadhar, over sixty people had spent four long days on three trees.

* *Now Mahemdavad, Bharuch and Vadodara*

Growing hungry and weary, children had begun falling off by the fifth day, and the current had sadly swept them off. More than 4,000 villages were entirely submerged, and over 75,000 houses had been washed away.

As such disturbing and heartbreaking news came in, it came to light that in less than a week the region had received 52 inches of rain, far more than its annual average of 30 inches. A fifty-year record of annual rainfall had been broken. Regions like Kheda had drowned entirely in water, and nothing but water could be seen for miles around. Soon, the rain led to other problems. There was an acute shortage of food grains and other daily essentials. The price of commodities had shot up.

Quickly mobilizing supplies of wheat, rice, sugar and kerosene, Patel had them dispatched to Kheda through a group of his volunteers. The material, the collector of Kheda later acknowledged, had reached the people there like a blessing from heaven.

Yet, even as Patel and his team of informal volunteers were out rescuing people, gathering information and sending relief, the efforts of the government moved at a snail's pace. Acknowledging Patel's remarkably swift action, the collector of Ahmedabad came to see him with a message from the Government of Bombay, requesting that Patel share the data he had gathered, to help them.

Not one to play politics over people's pain, Patel immediately shared all the information he had collected, cooperating fully in the government's belated efforts, without indulging in any kind of blame game or chest-thumping. 'It is not a political issue,' he said candidly, but a matter 'of compassion for human life'.

When asked if his name could be recommended for conferring an honour and title in recognition of his commendable relief work, he laughed as he turned down the offer and said, '...our delight is in doing service to the people; we are not anxious for publicity or fame.'

> Sardar is no man of words. He is a man of action. He does not look around or about himself when he has decided upon a course of action. He simply goes ahead. May he always be thus.

GANDHI, SPEAKING ABOUT PATEL IN 1940

17

THE HOUR OF RECKONING

Persist and you shall prevail

In 1928, the British government increases land revenue tax by 30 per cent in Bardoli, Gujarat. Having heard about Patel's successes in Borsad and his phenomenal relief work during the floods, farmers approach him to represent their cause against this unjust and arbitrary increase in taxes. 'Go back to Bardoli,' he tells the delegation, 'and find out if the people are prepared to put up a fight...if so, I am willing to come.' Ultimately, not only does Patel get involved, but he also becomes the leader of the historic movement. It changes not just the political landscape, but also Patel's fate. It is Bardoli where Vallabhbhai Patel becomes Sardar Patel.

'Are you ready to sacrifice your possessions for this struggle?' Patel asked the large crowd that had gathered to listen to him in Bardoli.

'YES!' the people replied as one.

'Even your lives?'

'YES!' the chorus was louder.

'Ladies...the government may take away your cattle to punish you. Are you prepared to bear that pain?' hollered Patel into the megaphone.

'We are,' replied the women without flinching.

'What if your husbands pay up the tax out of fear?'

'We won't allow them into the house,' cried the women without another thought.

Satisfied that the ground was ripe for the struggle, Patel nodded. He had done extensive homework after personally meeting the leaders of seventy-nine villages in the district and come to the conclusion that the 30 per cent increase in tax imposed by the government was arbitrary and unjust. But he wanted to be doubly sure the people were prepared to fight it out.

Convinced now that the soil was fertile, he met Gandhi, his guru and guide. 'I have no doubt the cause is just,' declared Patel.

'There is nothing more to be considered then,' replied Gandhi. 'Victory to Gujarat!'

Over the next few weeks, Patel launched a satyagraha of epic proportions in Bardoli. A chain of command right from the top to the district level and from the district level to the village-cluster level was formed, down to every village. Two hundred and fifty volunteers worked around the clock to manage the movement. A network of informers was deployed to gather intelligence. Five thousand students were asked to miss their classes and participate in the satyagraha. Fifteen thousand handbills were printed and distributed. Seven motor cars were made available for quick transport. Booths and camps were set up in public places to inform and organize. Public kitchens served hot food to agitators. Folk singers carried the message of resistance from village to village. 'Wake up, brave fighters; the battle drums have sounded!' they sang in songs composed for the satyagraha. Imams delivering sermons in mosques during Ramzan preached about the struggle. No stone was left unturned.

'If you make up your minds that you will not give one pie (a small unit of currency), whatever the government may do, however many confiscations it may carry out, however many fields it may seize, the government will not be able to collect the revised land revenue...' he told farmers. The people of Bardoli responded to Patel in full measure, refusing to pay the tax under any circumstances.

Patel travelled constantly, making speeches, mobilizing people, urging people of all castes and classes, and all religions and backgrounds to pledge their support. Remarkably, his call melted age-old fissures in society as Patidars and Baniyas, Christians and Muslims, upper castes and backward classes, anglicized Parsis and indigenous communities – they all came together as one.

This was not a question about money alone, said Patel, but a fight against oppression, a fight for self-respect. This was not just a question about one *taluka* or one tax, said Patel, but a turning point in India's struggle for freedom against the British. 'If you fail in this conflict,' Patel told the people, 'rest assured you will not be able to fight again for a hundred years.'

Given the size and the scale of the movement, the government began to panic. 'Patel has completely paralysed the revenue administration of the *taluka*,' reported *The Times of India* about the Bardoli Satyagraha. The administration that had until recently been praising Patel for his stellar work in organizing relief during the disastrous floods began heaping him with criticism.

The government tried every trick in the book to get farmers to pay – confiscating property, threatening farmers and offering a settlement. Local leader Ravishankar Maharaj was arrested. There were rumours that Patel himself may be arrested. But Sardar's fearless and bold leadership, along with his constant and compassionate support, ensured that the people stood firm. 'The government perhaps thought that by arresting Ravishankar Maharaj, they would be clipping my wings,' Patel declared, 'but let me assure them that my wings will grow afresh, as luxuriantly as grass grows in the rainy season.'

Further, as Gandhi's steadfast disciple, he made sure the fight adhered to the principle of non-violence. Ready as always with simple countryside analogies, Patel drew on tools in the blacksmith's workshop to explain the strategy. 'You are the hammer, and the government the angry red-hot metal,' he told the people. 'If the hammer stays cool, it can mould the iron into the desired shape.'

Finally, after months, the government relented – there would be no increase in tax, and all confiscated land would be returned. It was made clear that farmers needed to pay taxes only according to the old rate.

The farmers had won. Gujarat had won. Sardar had won. There were celebrations across Bardoli. When the fight had begun in April, it was helmed by Vallabhbhai Patel. By the time it had ended in August, its leader was Sardar Patel.

'I am going to Bardoli in response to the command of Sardar,' said Gandhi, implying Patel was the commander and Gandhi only a follower. For his part, though, Patel claimed no credit and felt acutely embarrassed with the praise that Gandhi showered upon him after the success. Likening himself to Eklavya from the *Mahabharata*, who had learnt archery by watching Dronacharya, he gave all credit to his guru Gandhi and the people of Bardoli for pulling off the historic victory.

> 'I doubt whether any leader has such a strong hold...as Vallabhbhai has over Gujarat. Vallabhbhai's personal influence in Gujarat is possibly greater even than Gandhi's.'
>
> SECRET GOVERNMENT COMMUNICATION BY A BRITISH OFFICER IN 1934

18

SERMON OF THE BUFFALOES

Find humour in the mundane

In 1928, a historic farmers' movement is launched in the district of Bardoli in Gujarat to oppose unjust taxes imposed by the government. Leading the satyagraha, Patel travels from village to village, addressing farmers, encouraging them to resist the government's harsh measures. It is a hard fight during the intense summer months against a ruthless administration. But even during a serious struggle, Patel is able to harness the power of his wit that brings a smile to the suffering farmer's face.

In consultation with Patel, the farmers of Bardoli had thought of a clever strategy to resist the government – one he had tried and succeeded with in Borsad earlier. A volunteer was deputed to sit atop a tree on the outskirts of every village and keep vigil. As soon as a tax official was spotted advancing towards the village from a distance, the volunteer was to beat a drum to alert the residents.

The farmers were then to take their cattle, lock their homes and quickly leave the village from the other end. As a result, when the tax officials arrived, they would find deserted houses and an abandoned village, forcing them to go back empty-handed, without attaching property or recovering the unpaid tax. The farmers would return to the village at night because the law prohibited tax officers from attaching properties after sunset.

To counter this, the government issued an order prohibiting the beating of drums at public places. No drums were to be beaten on roads and squares, at protests and gatherings.

When he addressed a meeting in Valod village, Patel took the prohibition order head-on and mocked this bizarre government order. 'Now we are to stop beating drums and blowing conches,' he told the crowd gathered to listen to him. 'The government is terrified by our drums, as if the empire will crumble down if our children beat drums. Such a great government with so much artillery, guns and such a big army is terrified by drums and firecracker blasts. What a terror!'

'BGHHHHHHHH-MHHHOOOO-GGGHHHHHH'

Just then, a dozen odd buffaloes that had been forcibly taken from some farmers to recover the unpaid tax and confined in the backyard of Valod Police Station bellowed loudly. The buffaloes had not been given fodder or water for some days, causing great distress to their owners, for whom their cattle were as dear as family.

'Listen to these bellowing buffaloes,' Sardar said, latching on to the opportunity. 'Reporters, you must report that the buffaloes caged in Valod Police Station delivered a discourse to protest against the government. The government is already terrified of our drums. Now how will it withstand the protest of these buffaloes?'

The crowd laughed, forgetting momentarily the gloom they felt over the loss of their beloved cattle in several unlawful raids over the last few weeks, despite the clever tactics they'd employed. To help them intimidate the people, the police had even hired muscular Pathan men, who were found marching about the countryside, randomly confiscating cattle. So common had the sight become that a local leader had parodied the famous lines of the poet Lord Alfred Tennyson from 'The Charge of the Light Brigade':

'Pathans to the left of them.
Pathans to the right of them,
Pathans in front of them,
Police at the tail of them,
Marched the Buffalo Brigade!'

'It is due to Bardoli that petty peons and Pathans, for whom a bullock-cart was a luxury, are now having joyrides in government motor cars!' joked Patel sardonically, to boost the morale of the people. 'All this while, the government has simply ignored you people...now even the District Superintendent finds time to pay you a visit in the scorching summer. It is no small honour, this.'

As Patel spoke, the buffaloes confined in the police station bellowed again, as if they too were applauding Patel's speech, making the people laugh some more. It had been a hard few months since they had all taken the pledge to refuse to pay the higher rate of tax that the government had arbitrarily imposed upon them. Some of them had lost their cattle; others had lost their land. Worse, they had no

PATEL SKILLFULLY TRANSFORMS THE BELLOWING OF BUFFALOES INTO A POLITICAL STATEMENT

idea how much longer this struggle would go on or if there was going to be any light at all at the end of this dark tunnel. Laughter had not been heard around here for months.

'These buffaloes, I tell you, are as bad as the drums,' Patel said. 'They are bellowing themselves hoarse to tell you the condition of the British Empire...if you haven't understood already.

'Listen to these buffaloes!' he continued. 'They are telling you that justice has vanished from this empire, and buffaloes are being punished and imprisoned for the protest made by humans. After fifteen days of hunger and thirst, buffaloes are being put on trial and sentenced to death.'

'BHHAAAA-MHHHAAAA.' The buffaloes grunted and snorted some more, as if relieved to find a sympathetic voice.

'Listen to these bellowing buffaloes...' roared Sardar amid much laughter and mirth. 'Listen as they cry out for justice against the mighty British government.'

Forgetting their worries for a few moments, the farmers laughed heartily, appreciating Patel's uncanny ability to animate ordinary events and bring them alive with his humour.

> 'Vallabhbhai had a way with peasants and the skill to elicit facts from them.'

RAOJIBHAI PATEL, PATEL'S COLLEAGUE
IN THE KHEDA SATYAGRAHA IN 1918

19

PLAIN HONESTY

Choose facts over foolery

In the 1900s, great value is placed upon formality, courtesy and propriety. As someone who wore his heart on his sleeve and always called a spade a spade, Patel breaks out of that mould. When Patel speaks, he gives expression to his mind without undue concern for formality and political correctness. A person of this community or that, friend or foe, nobody is spared his blunt and forthright honesty.

In December 1929, Patel was on a tour of Bihar, where he was called upon to address farmers. 'Why do you keep your women behind a purdah?' he said, taking head-on the practice among Muslims. 'Who are these ladies? Your mothers, sisters, wives.' He was unapologetic in challenging traditions that restricted women.

Later, he took on those raising a hue and cry about Christian conversions by honestly showing upper-caste Hindus the mirror. 'If you had not treated the untouchables as inferior beings, would this have happened?'

Speaking of malpractices like child marriage, he took on the priestly class and strongly admonished those who, in the name of religion, got people to marry children of tender age.

In January 1948, addressing Muslims in Lucknow who had expressed loyalty to Pakistan in a public meeting in the months following Partition, he said, 'I want to tell you very frankly that you cannot ride two horses. Select one horse. Those who want to go to Pakistan can go there and live in peace.'

At the same time, Patel warned those threatening Muslims as well. 'You have just now heard people shouting that Muslims should be removed from India. Those who do so have gone mad with anger. Even a lunatic is better than a person mad with rage.' While the former, he said, could be treated and perhaps cured, the latter were a menace and a danger to stability and peace.

Patel was equally terse with leaders of Hindu groups. He rejected their narrow interpretation of Hinduism, saying, 'If you think that you are the only custodians of Hinduism, you are mistaken. Hinduism preaches a broader outlook.'

In another instance, Vallabhbhai said, 'If you think that you can go on constantly troubling loyal Muslims because they happen to be Muslims, then our freedom is not worthwhile.'

Putting the onus of peace on the Hindu majority, he said, 'What we want is heart-unity, not patched-up paper-unity that will break at the slightest strain. That unity can only come when the majority takes courage in both hands and is prepared to change places with the minority. This would be the highest wisdom.'

Being a man of action, sloganeering and speech-making did not impress Patel. He called out socialists and communists for causing disruption by encouraging labourers to go on strike, and urged them instead to make a more constructive contribution.

Sardar Patel's no-nonsense approach and unflinching honesty spared no one.

> I am a frank man – I say bitter things to Hindus and Muslims alike.

SARDAR PATEL, SPEAKING ABOUT A SPEECH HE DELIVERED IN LUCKNOW IN JANUARY 1948

20

IRONCLAD

Contentment is a state of mind

It is early 1930; Gandhi is about to set off from Sabarmati Ashram for Dandi (Gujarat) to launch a march against the colonial government's unjust salt tax. Alongside, Sardar has taken up the task of educating people about Gandhi's salt satyagraha in areas around the proposed route.

On 7 March 1930, Sardar travels to Ras village, where thousands have gathered to hear him. Anticipating trouble, the local magistrate orders Sardar not to make a speech, but Patel is not going to obey. Upon hearing this, the magistrate arrests him. After a sham of a trial in Borsad, Sardar is sentenced to three months in prison, and a fine of five hundred rupees is imposed upon him for delivering a speech that he never made. His friends and associates – Mahadev Desai and Acharya Kripalani – go to meet him at Sabarmati Jail to enquire about him.

'How are you keeping?' asked Mahadev Desai, worried about Gandhi's commander.

'I am perfectly happy,' smiled Sardar, holding up his hands in contentment.

'Are you able to sleep?' Acharya Kripalani's eyebrows furrowed as he cast a furtive glance at the prison cells visible in the large courtyard behind the meeting room.

'To be honest,' chuckled Sardar, 'I was afraid I wouldn't be able to sleep at all, but fortunately there has been no difficulty. They lock up the cell for the night at 5.30 p.m. and even earlier at 3.30 p.m. on Sundays. I have been sleeping like a log.'

'Ah, so you have a bed?' asked Desai, adjusting his glasses.

'I have a blanket,' smiled Sardar, saying no more.

The visitors exchanged glances. They both knew Sardar well and were all too familiar with his habit of taking difficulties in his stride without a murmur or complaint. He was having trouble using the single latrine meant for dozens of prisoners and couldn't get himself to use the pot in public view to urinate. There was not enough water to bathe every day, and he was not used to sleeping on the floor.

'What about the food?' asked Desai. He had been told Patel routinely skipped breakfast for fear of getting dysentery from the *jowar* gruel served each morning and had suffered from indigestion. 'What do you eat?'

'Ah! The food...' Sardar rubbed his palms together as if he were anticipating a feast, throwing an all-knowing glance at the jailer sitting at the other end of the room. 'It's as good or as bad as one can expect,' he said, shrugging, before bursting into loud laughter. 'Don't worry about my food. I assure you I can live on air for three months.'

'No...seriously...I heard you don't eat the gruel they serve for breakfast,' Acharya Kripalani pressed him for details. 'Do you eat lunch?'

'Hmm...' nodded Sardar. 'We are given *jowar* roti with dal or vegetables in the afternoons.'

'And you manage to chew the roti?' asked Desai, his hand tapping his right cheek to signify the toothache he knew Sardar was suffering from.

'Oh, I just soak the roti in water and get along splendidly,' laughed Sardar. 'I tell you, you need not worry at all about my food,' he assured them yet again.

'Do you need us to...uh...get you anything?' asked Desai.

'Maybe some soap and shaving material...'

'Razors are not allowed inside,' interjected the jailer from his desk promptly. 'But you can ask for a shave, and it will be given to you.'

'I know what kind of shave you will give,' scoffed Sardar. 'Why not give me the razor instead, and I will shave the other inmates?' he suggested. 'Seriously – it will also give me something to do.'

The jailer turned back to the register on his desk without making a reply.

Mahadev Desai placed a gentle hand on Sardar's shoulder, his eyes filled with admiration. Here was a man who had given up a plush life of crisp suits and expensive cigars and thrown himself into the freedom struggle. It was taking a toll on the fifty-five-year-old, he could tell. But Sardar was not a man to mope and moan. Even while serving a jail sentence for something he had not done, not a single complaint escaped his lips. Instead, he was laughing away his woes and was ready to serve other prisoners as a simple barber so that he could be useful and productive.

'Don't worry about me,' Sardar patted Desai, a contented smile lighting up his face. 'I am as happy as a bird.'

> Don't worry about my health. I am taking good care of it. There is much left for me to do in this world, and I have faith that I will see the completion of what I have taken in hand.

SARDAR PATEL TO GHULAM RASOOL QURESHI, A FEW WEEKS AFTER RELEASE FROM YERWADA JAIL, WHERE HE WAS IN POOR HEALTH AND LOST NEARLY TEN KILOS

21

SARDAR FOREVER

Earn your honours

During the Bardoli Satyagraha of 1928, Vallabhbhai Patel starts getting addressed as 'Sardar' by the people. However, not everyone is pleased with this title. In October 1931, the home secretary of Bombay corrects his colleague in New Delhi regarding the letters being written to Patel: 'The title of Sardar, which you are using in writing to Mr Vallabhbhai Patel...is not one which he has a right to use. The Sardars of Gujarat are an order created by the government. They consist of gentlemen, usually large landowners, who have rendered distinguished service.' *It is not just the British but members of Patel's own party too who oppose this prefix being added before his name.*

'T*ch,*' sighed Congress leader Jivatram Kripalani. 'This is Patel...' he pointed to the moustached man standing by his side. 'Sardar Patel...'

'Sorry, sir,' the volunteer shrugged, 'no entry without an identity card.'

'Listen, boy...' said Kripalani, his eyes on the sea of people pouring into the large pandal for the annual Congress session taking place in Calcutta.* 'This is the man who led the historic satyagraha in Bardoli against the British...'

'*Ami jani na aapni ke* (I don't know who you are),' the young volunteer posted at the gate said with a wobble of his palm. 'I don't know him. Now please move aside and allow others to enter.'

Kripalani nudged Patel. 'Check again.'

Upturning the pockets of his waistcoat, Patel shrugged. 'I've forgotten the ID card in my room.'

'Please, son...' Kripalani turned once again to the young man. 'You don't understand. This here is Sardar Vallabhbhai Patel, a respected Congress leader from Gujarat whose successful movement in Bardoli has become legend... You are—'

'If you don't have your ID card, please step away,' repeated the volunteer sternly, totally unimpressed.

'You don't seem to be aware of who he is,' Kripalani advanced toward the boy. 'You can ask anyone—'

Patel placed a hand on his friend's shoulder. 'Never mind,' he stopped him. 'I'll go back...'

* *Now Kolkata*

That day, Patel returned to his quarters without attending the session. But the next day was a wholly different affair. From then on, neither the volunteer at the gate nor any other would say that they did not know or recognize Patel.

'The next item on our agenda today,' a committee member of the party read from a list in his hand, 'is to felicitate Shri Vallabhbhai Patel for his remarkable work in Bardoli...'

'Hear, hear!' the committee members cheered, welcoming the motion.

'I have no opposition to the congratulatory resolution,' said an attendee, 'but what is this prefix *Sardar* that has been added before his name?'

'It is what the people of Bardoli call him,' replied the member proposing the resolution.

'But what use have we for such feudal honours?' said the protester. 'We must shun them. Class titles must find no place in our language.'

'I second that,' said a voice.

'Me too,' said another, as more committee members backed the removal of the word *Sardar* from the text.

Kripalani pursed his lips, recalling how Patel, a man at the forefront of the farmers' resistance at Bardoli, had been lovingly bestowed that title. It was not a hereditary title he was born into, nor one conferred by the government in exchange for loyalty to the British. Instead, it was a title he had earned from the grassroots, from the people, from inspired village folk who had spontaneously begun calling him their leader in the summer of 1928.

'Let's speak to Sardar...'

'Did you hear Sardar? His speech was fiery.'

'We've got to tell Sardar...'

That was how Vallabhbhai Patel had become Sardar Patel. Not by birth or inheritance; not with a badge or medal. But with love and respect.

Tuning out of his memories, Kripalani turned his eyes to the stage, where a modified version of the resolution to felicitate Patel was being moved after commending him for the historic battle and monumental triumph at Bardoli. The word *Sardar* had been edited out of the text. Even so, people had other ideas.

'Where is Sardar?' asked someone in the crowd, keen to see the leader from Gujarat after hearing about the success of the Bardoli satyagraha.

'Sardar Patel is sitting there,' replied another, pointing toward the corner where all the delegates from Gujarat were seated.

'Sardar, show yourself...' A clamour began around the stoic figure sitting cross-legged on the ground.

Standing up, Patel folded his hands in greeting.

'Sardar, up on the platform,' said someone in the crowd.

'Yes! We want to see Sardar Patel.'

Conveying his unwillingness to go on stage with a wave of his hands, Patel sat down. But people rushed towards him, pulling him up against his will.

Folding his hands, he bowed before the gathering as the Congress pandal resounded with rapturous applause.

'Sardar, you must say a few words...' A microphone was thrust before him.

Reluctantly, Patel made a short speech. 'I thank you for having congratulated the farmers of Bardoli. If you are genuinely appreciative of what they have done, I hope you will follow in their footsteps.'

Accepting the appreciation and the resolution, he descended the stage, conveying clearly in his brief address that words mattered less to him than deeds.

The prefix *Sardar* had been deleted from the piece of paper and the Congress resolution. But it could not be erased from people's lips and hearts. How long could naysayers resist when even Gandhi had long accepted it, saying, 'Long live Sardar to fight many a good fight!'

> 'There should be no need to speak of our virtues. They speak for themselves.'

SARDAR PATEL, SPEAKING AT KARAMSAD IN MARCH 1942

22

THE WIT WITHIN

Laugh through life's troubles

Between 1932 and 1933, Patel is in Yerwada Jail with Gandhi and Mahadev Desai. During his imprisonment, Gandhi goes on a fast to protest the government's plan to allot separate electorates for Muslims and Dalits. As his health deteriorates, many are worried. Under severe pressure because of Gandhi's declining condition, Babasaheb Ambedkar, leader of the Dalit movement, comes to jail to settle the issue (what becomes known as the Poona Pact), and the government relents. Gandhi finally calls off the fast.

Everyone heaved a sigh of relief. Gandhi had finally decided to bring his fast to an end. Inmates crowded around the mango tree in the prison yard, under which Gandhi's wife Kasturba was holding a glass of orange juice to Bapu's parched lips.

Seven days ago, Gandhi had given up food to protest against the government's decision to have separate electorates for Muslims, Sikhs and the 'untouchables'.

Despite being in jail, Gandhi had decided to take on the administration with that unique weapon called *fasting*.

Having heard of the fast over the last week, the world outside the prison gates had swung into action. Thousands had vowed to give up orthodox discriminatory practices. Temples were thrown open to people of all castes. A League for the Abolition of Untouchability had been formed. Renowned writer Rabindranath Tagore had come to visit Gandhi. Ambedkar had agreed to renegotiate terms. Kasturba was granted special permission to meet Gandhi in jail. With tensions rising, the government had yielded. After being shown the official decision, Gandhi had agreed to end his fast.

'I shall eat something after a sponge bath,' said Gandhi in a voice so feeble that he was barely audible.

Several inmates rushed to fetch towels for Gandhi. The sooner Bapu could eat something, the sooner their worries would end.

'I would like to have an account of the towels,' said Gandhi after he had broken his fast.

'Ba, is your husband not tyrannical?' Patel said huffily, turning to Kasturba as he sat tensely by Gandhi's side. *Did Bapu have any idea how anxious they had all been about his condition?* Usually most meticulous about keeping account, it baffled him that Gandhi should worry about the count of towels when they had all been worried sick for his life.

'Why should I give you an account?' Vallabhbhai said, turning back to Gandhi. 'We thought we had lost you. We had no idea you were going to come back and hound us for accounts...so we didn't keep any!'

Gandhi could only smile. Noting the banter in his diary, where he recorded every detail of Gandhi's life, Mahadev Desai turned back a few pages, his eyes falling upon a humorous exchange between Gandhi and Patel before they were jailed.

During the Bardoli Satyagraha a year ago, it was being said that Sardar may be arrested for encouraging farmers to defy the government by not paying taxes. Gandhi had written to Patel, saying, 'There are rumours that you may be arrested.'

Not in the least perturbed, Patel had remarked, 'Why should I be arrested? There is hardly any chance. The poor buffalo at least fetches a few rupees. I would fetch nothing if attached and sold.'

Recalling that conversation with a smile, Desai put away his diary and rose to make his bed. 'Bapu has very few teeth left,' he could hear Patel mumbling away in the adjoining cell as he prepared Gandhi's *datun* with a twig from the neem tree. 'Still he keeps on brushing them.'

With a chuckle, Desai rolled out his bed, flooded by a torrent of memories.

Some weeks ago, Gandhi had asked the prison major for a lighter cot so he could carry it into the veranda to sleep at night. A coir charpoy had arrived a few days later, much to Gandhi's joy and Patel's dismay.

'How can you sleep on that?' Patel had protested.

'Why not?' Gandhi had quipped. 'See how clean we can keep this cot.'

'You are a very strange person,' Patel had thrown up his hands. 'All we have to do is to place four coconuts at each corner, and it will resemble a plank to carry the dead! We cannot have anything to do with such an inauspicious cot.'

'A mattress with cotton will collect dust, and it cannot be washed,' Gandhi had argued. 'This, on the other hand, can be washed by just pouring water on it. It is light and easier to maintain.'

'Give the cotton mattress to the *dhobi*... He will wash it for you.'

'Why the trouble? This one, I can wash myself.'

'The coir cot will be full of bugs.'

'I am going to sleep on this. You may not care much for such a cot, but I remember that in my childhood, this is the kind of cot we used. My mother used to rub ginger on it.'

'What is that supposed to mean?' Mahadev Desai had interjected with a question.

'When you want to make ginger pickles, instead of cleaning the ginger with a knife, if you rub it on coir threads, all the skin will peel off easily,' Gandhi had explained.

'Bah!' Patel had laughed. 'In exactly the same way, the skin over your handful of bones will also peel off. That is precisely the reason I ask you to replace the coir with cotton.'

As Desai lay down, he recalled a newspaper report a few months ago that had stated that the government did not intend to release Gandhi.

Upon reading this, Gandhi had casually remarked, 'Look, didn't I tell you that I'd be in jail for five years?'

Astounded at Gandhi's nonchalance, Patel had responded, 'You behave like a thick-skinned person who, when told that a babul tree had grown on his back, replied saying, "That is very good. It will now give me shade."'

A few days later, Congressman Srinivasa Sastri wrote to Gandhi to enquire about his well-being. 'Sardar Vallabhbhai is with me,' replied Gandhi. 'His jokes make me laugh until I can laugh no more, not once but several times every day.'

Patel's wry humour was the saving grace for not just Gandhi and Desai in Yerwada but also anyone else who ever found themselves imprisoned with him. Jailed together in 1942 with Sardar after the Quit India Movement, Congress leader Pattabhi Sitaramayya said of the three years he spent in prison with Patel: 'He chokes you with laughter by a play of sharp and incisive wit.'

> "One of the greatest joys of my life was that I had the opportunity of staying in prison with Sardar."
>
> MAHATMA GANDHI

23

NO IMPOSITION

Be stern, not strict

On 11 January 1909, Patel's wife, Jhaverba, dies following an intestinal surgery. Vallabhbhai, only thirty-four years old then, finds himself a single parent to two young children – Mani and Dahya, aged five and four respectively. Initially away in England for further studies, then busy with his legal practice in Ahmedabad, followed by several years of devoted service to the country, a large part of which is spent in jail, finding time for the family is challenging for him.

Patel had lost his wife suddenly at a very young age, so he could understand the anguish his son Dahyabhai was going through. It wasn't easy coping with the untimely death of one's partner, but all the relatives pestering the boy to remarry didn't make things any easier. Although separated from his children by many hundreds of miles and high prison walls, he was with them in spirit and could only hope his words would comfort them.

'Tell those asking about Dahyabhai's remarriage politely but firmly,' he wrote to his daughter Maniben, 'that this is a matter for him to decide. He is an adult and knows his own mind. There is no need for anyone to give him any advice.'

Dahyabhai was young, not even thirty. His wife, Yashoda, had recently passed away, and Patel knew that grief was not something that could magically vanish.

'People ask because that is our society's custom,' he pacified his daughter, who was growing annoyed at having to deal with a barrage of questions from relatives. 'Why should we take that amiss? It is difficult to say what Dahyabhai will do. It will take some time before the wound heals.'

He shared his thoughts with his son too. It was for Dahyabhai to make a decision; he would not encroach upon his son's domain. 'Think over the question of your remarriage… What has to be settled first is what you want.'

Through friends and well-wishers who visited Patel in jail, he learnt that his son was having problems – with his landlord, with his cousin and with others. 'The tone of your business is stiff and cold…which might offend,' Patel pointed out to his son. 'It is not desirable that even in official correspondence, you should say anything which may hurt anyone's feelings or increase his hostility.'

Recollecting his own youth, Patel told his son of a time when he too had been stiff and harsh as a young man but had grown to regret his ways later, urging Dahyabhai not to make the same mistakes. 'We must do what we think is right, but our independence does not mean that we should treat other people with contempt.'

Having heard about trouble between his son and nephew, he wrote, 'I see the two of you cannot get on together. Both of you should therefore separate. If two people cannot live amicably together, it is far better for them to live apart.'

His son Dahyabhai wrote back, complaining about the boy's mother. Patel had a simple response. 'Even if what you say is true, I believe your thinking is faulty. However bad his mother was, why should you blame the boy? If we behave exactly as other people do, what is the difference between them and ourselves?'

Although he was addressing his son in an age when the father's word was to be obeyed without question, Patel repeatedly urged his son to consider his advice thoughtfully before coming to a decision: 'I would like you to think over what I tell you carefully, and if you agree with me, try to act accordingly.'

'We must not allow any matter to worry us unduly,' he summarized his life's philosophy. 'Things do not always happen as we want them to... We must hesitate or be afraid only of doing the wrong thing or committing a sin. Otherwise, we must fear nothing... Everyone carries his own fate with himself.'

> 'There is a limit even to the advice one may give when the person concerned is grown up.'

SARDAR PATEL, IN A LETTER DATED 17 FEBRUARY 1932 FROM YERWADA JAIL ON A MATTER CONCERNING AN ERRANT NEPHEW

24

RAW AND REAL

Call a spade a spade

From January 1932 to July 1934, Sardar is imprisoned in Yerwada Jail. For much of that time, Gandhi is also with him, and the bond between the two grows into something special. One of their other companions in jail is Mahadev Desai, who keeps a meticulous diary of their days together – serious discussions, daily routine and light banter. One day, disturbed by a scathing article, Gandhi is trying to write a response to it.

Sardar turned to the clock in the corridor and then to Gandhi sitting cross-legged on the floor, bent over his writing pad. It had been nearly an hour; Gandhi had been at it without a break – drafting a seemingly endless letter to Lord Sankey in the British Government about his article, which Gandhi had found wholly offensive.

'Tch,' Sardar clicked his tongue as he sat down by his notebook to start his lesson for the day. Nudged by Gandhi, he had begun learning Sanskrit in jail and was growing to enjoy it immensely, throwing around proverbs by the dozen whenever the occasion demanded it. This was a much better use of jail time, in his opinion, than wasting precious hours responding to cynical critics.

Despite all the changes Gandhi had brought about in Sardar's behaviour and attire, this attitude was always at the very core of Sardar's personality. Not too long ago, when he had been arguing a criminal case in the sessions court in Kheda, which was labelled a criminal district by government officials, he had fearlessly taken on the judge himself.

While appearing in a murder case on behalf of two accused brothers, against whom no evidence had been found, Patel had not hesitated to call out the judge's bias when he denied them bail.

'I regret very much to note that no accused from Kheda gets a fair trial in this court,' he had said bluntly. 'If there is insufficient evidence, it is suggested that the accused, being a Kheda man, must have tampered with it. Since the district is considered to be criminal, whether there is evidence or not, it is thought that the accused must be convicted.'

While all this was true, nobody had ever dared to say so before a judge, most certainly not in open court.

Taken aback, the judge had taken a few moments to gather his thoughts. 'Uh...Mr Patel,' he had said, 'you are obviously in an excited mood when you make such a serious allegation against the court.' But not having any reasonable explanation to give, he had adjourned the court for half an hour and gone into his chamber.

Having refused bail only moments ago, the judge had returned to grant bail to the accused brothers. In the days to come, they were both acquitted of the charge. This was Sardar's way – plain-speaking and forthrightness.

Turning back from old memories to the wall clock again, Sardar cast another look at Gandhi, who was still labouring over his letter. Gandhi, being Gandhi, was carefully crafting his arguments in an orderly manner, pointing out the various flaws in his opponent's article. Sardar, being who he was, shook his head in irritation. 'Why all this toil and trouble?' he said. 'Instead of writing such a long letter,' he said to Gandhi, 'why don't you simply tell the man he's a liar and get done with it?'

Making an entry in his daily diary, Mahadev Desai grinned at Sardar's blunt style. Why beat around the bush when the truth was so evident? Clearly, Sardar felt no need to window-dress his real feelings and package them with pretence within the folds of formality.

> He meant what he said and said what he meant.

LIAQUAT ALI KHAN, FIRST PRIME MINISTER OF PAKISTAN, SPEAKING ABOUT SARDAR PATEL

25

STANDING TALL

Respect yourself first

In 1933, Patel is in Nasik Jail when he receives the news that his older brother Vithalbhai has passed away in Geneva, Switzerland, and that his body is being sent back to India. Although Patel does not ask to be released for his brother's funeral, friends request a temporary discharge on his behalf. The government says it is agreeable to release Patel for forty-eight hours, but only if he adheres to certain conditions.*

Pressing two fingers into the corner of his eyes, Patel slid against the wall of his cell in Nasik Jail, where he had been imprisoned for some months now. Life here had tested him in every way. He had been kept in solitary confinement, denied newspapers and forbidden to meet other prisoners. Despite repeated medical attention, his nose was giving him hell. But all those had been light crosses for him to bear. This news was a mighty blow.

* *Now Nasik*

His dear brother Vithalbhai had breathed his last. That too in a strange land so many miles away, without family to care for him. *How must he have spent his final days? Had he been yearning for home?* These thoughts tormented Patel.

'I hear Subhas was with Vithalbhai…' Fellow inmate and long-time associate Chandulal Desai placed a sympathetic hand on Vallabhbhai's shoulder. Desai had worked with Patel during the Bardoli Satyagraha, and Patel was grateful for his presence in jail with him at this difficult time. 'I hear Bose looked after him when he was unwell. And that he is sending Vithalbhai's body to India.'

Patel nodded. His differences with both Subhas Chandra Bose and Vithalbhai had created a yawning gap between them over the years. Especially after they had both issued a joint statement from Austria some months ago declaring that Gandhi's leadership had failed. And yet, Patel had never allowed political tussles to mar his personal relationship with his brother. In fact, he had written to Vithalbhai several times from jail, despite their differing political views. But he wasn't sure the letters had even reached his brother.

'Do you wish to apply to the government to be temporarily released for Vithalbhai's funeral to perform the last rites?' asked Desai. 'He has no children.'

Patel shook his head. He hated the thought of bending before the British. This was a personal matter. He could not bow before the British or beg with folded hands and ask for favours. 'No…' he shook his head. 'I will not apply.'

Patel had, after all, led many a struggle against the colonial Raj. He had repeatedly urged the people to think of the fight against the British in moral and not monetary terms. He had stressed on the importance of self-respect, a value that his mentor, Gandhi, had tried so hard to inculcate into India's masses.

Sardar himself had spoken about it repeatedly. Back in Champaran in 1929, he evoked a sense of self-esteem and pride in the humble farmer: 'You are the people who give food to the world. You live by the sweat of your toil, and not merely that; it is on the results of your toil that most others live. The world cannot do without you.... the rest are parasites. You are the food giver. If you are idle, the whole world will starve... I resent the description of the peasant as a mere wretched creature... If anyone has the right to walk with his head erect...it is the peasant.'

Speaking elsewhere, he had said, 'You have forgotten your dignity as human beings; you have lost your sense of self-respect... Anybody may oppress you in any way he likes...like your own bullocks when they are heartlessly overloaded and hard-driven in the hot burning sun.'

In every speech and struggle, Patel had laid stress on self-respect. *How could he not follow his own honour code now?*

While Patel did not apply for special permission, upon the request of some of his friends, the government agreed to conditionally release Patel for forty-eight hours, provided he undertook not to make political speeches, and to present himself for arrest at an agreed place and time. Patel had not seen his brother for over a year. The desire to see him one last time rose like a wave. But letting out a deep sigh, he threw back his head: 'I do not believe in asking for special permission from the government. Why should I place myself under special obligation to them?'

Ultimately, Vallabhbhai's son Dahyabhai performed Vithalbhai's last rites. A huge procession took place in Bombay in his honour. Vallabhbhai's daughter Maniben, who was out of jail, was there. Sarojini Naidu made a moving speech. But Vallabhbhai would not attend it. Not at the cost of his self-respect.

> 'I cannot purchase my liberty at the sacrifice of my honour and self-respect.'
>
> PATEL'S RESPONSE TO THE GOVERNMENT IN 1933

26

UNBREAKABLE

Don't play the victim card

Patel is arrested in January 1932 without a trial or a fixed sentence for resisting the government. He has only recently undergone a nasal surgery. While in jail, the condition worsens considerably; he finds it hard to breathe and impossible to sleep. However, getting any kind of relief is not straightforward.

'This is not looking good,' said the medical officer of Yerwada Jail after examining Patel's nose. 'It may need to be operated on again.'

'I met my doctor, Dr Deshmukh, sometime before I was arrested,' replied Patel, pressing a towel against his bleeding nose. 'He had advised a surgery back then. But it was a busy time...I was not able to spare a fortnight. I got it attended to and cauterized the day before my arrest.'

'You were brought to jail in an open jeep, weren't you?' asked the doctor.

Patel nodded.

'Looks like the long ride from Bombay to Poona in windy conditions has made it worse.'

'I am in a lot of pain, doctor,' Patel said, wincing. 'I have had it operated on once before, but as you say, the journey has made things worse.'

'A nasal surgery is very delicate,' advised the jail doctor. 'You need to take great care.'

'I wish to have the operation only if all the necessary facilities are available,' said Patel, quite certain he wanted it only in the presence of his capable and experienced doctor.

'The government may agree to allow the operation at Sassoon Hospital in Poona...'

'No,' said Patel, 'I need my doctors who know my condition to perform the surgery so that there is less risk.'

'Mr Patel,' sighed the prison doctor, 'the Inspector General of Prisons will permit the surgery only if it is in Poona. I can put in a request that you wish for it to be conducted by your own doctor from Bombay.'

'And how is Dr Deshmukh to keep coming up and down from Bombay to Poona through my surgery and treatment? It would be most inconvenient for him,' said Patel. 'Besides, he may not be given the facilities he needs here.'

Soon after, Patel was examined by the civil surgeon of Sassoon Hospital and by the nose specialist, Dr Mandlik. 'The operation is not an urgent one...' they said after their examination. They also declared that if he wanted his own doctor, he would have to find the money for it, and if anything went wrong, the government would in no way be responsible.

Swallowing the bitter pill, Patel decided to bear the pain and wait it out. But his condition only worsened. Having heard about his deteriorating state of health, a concerned Gandhi wrote to him. Patel asked him not to worry.

Patel was in a quandary. For over a year now, he had been treated by the jail doctors, and there had been no improvement whatsoever. While his own doctor was saying the surgery was essential, Dr Mandlik was saying it wasn't. Even other doctors Patel consulted – Dr Ansari and Dr Shah – had all advised him to undergo the operation in Bombay by a competent surgeon.

As his condition continued to worsen, the government allowed Sardar to be examined again by his doctors, Dr Deshmukh and Dr Damini, who reiterated that he needed to be operated upon immediately, followed by more procedures. They also advised for the delicate surgery to be done in Bombay, as special care would be necessary after the operation.

Their report was rejected by the government, which insisted on the Sassoon Hospital in Poona.

'My doctors cannot spare six weeks' stay in Poona,' replied Patel. 'My pain is unbearable, but that will have to be borne until the government is advised by its own doctors that my operation is essential.'

Meanwhile, he had been shifted from one jail to another and kept in solitary confinement. 'We won't lose heart no matter what is done,' he had said to the superintendent, 'put us in a dark cell if you want.' His nose was making it impossible to sleep at night. Unable to lie down, he would sit for hours until the painful attacks subsided. His letters to his children and friends were being scanned and censored by the jail authorities. Other prisoners were not allowed to meet him. In November 1932, he received the devastating news that his mother had passed away. About a year later, he lost his brother. He bore it all, not once making a fuss or taking advantage of his plight to gain sympathy or special treatment.

Despite a year of suffering, the last thing Patel wanted was to ask for the government's favour. And he most certainly did not want Gandhi to plead with the government on his account.

Ultimately, Patel would not be able to have the surgery that he needed while he was in jail. It would be two long years of sleepless nights and excruciating pain, borne for much part in loneliness. It was only in 1935, after he was out of jail, that Patel was finally operated upon and was able to get some relief.

> Remember that sunset is followed by sunrise, and a dark night is followed by a bright dawn... There is no reason to feel either helpless or hopeless.

SARDAR PATEL, IN A LETTER DATED 29 DECEMBER 1933 TO A VOLUNTEER OF KASTURBA SEVASHRAM

27

PATIENCE PAYS

Sometimes, restraint is the best response

In 1937, Parsi lawyer Khurshed F. Nariman, who heads the Congress in Bombay city, wishes to be the prime minister of Bombay (heads of provinces were called prime ministers back then). However, he loses the vote, and Balasaheb Kher is unanimously elected as the leader by the legislators. Patel is the chairman of the Congress Parliamentary Board, and an annoyed Nariman launches a virulent campaign against him, claiming that Sardar Patel was the reason for his defeat.

Sadashiv Patil, secretary of the Congress in Bombay, pursed his lips as he turned toward Patel. Poring over a newspaper, Sardar was dabbing his moist eyes, hurt by the all-out attack on him in the media.

A few days ago, Congress members of the Bombay State Legislature had voted to choose their leader. Although Khurshed Nariman was in the fray, Balasaheb Kher had been elected by a unanimous vote. Nariman, a big name with a huge following in Bombay city, turned terribly bitter.

Almost immediately, the Bombay-based newspapers launched a concerted campaign in support of Nariman, who in turn had his guns trained on Patel.

Great injustice, the papers screamed, had been done to Mr Nariman. As chairman of the Congress Parliamentary Board, Sardar Patel had put improper pressure upon members of the Bombay Congress to influence their vote against him. Worse – that Sardar had been guided by communal bias in his preference for Kher over Nariman.

It hurt. It stung. Each one of the nasty barbs tore through Sardar's heart. The allegation that he had interfered in the election was distasteful. But the accusation that he had been guided by communal prejudice was painful beyond measure.

As the days wore on, although Patel remained silent, Nariman would not relent. Taking his attack up a notch, he shot off angry letters to Jawaharlal Nehru, the Congress president. He accused three others – Shankarrao Deo, Gangadharrao Deshpande and Achyut Patwardhan. All of them, he said, had worked against him at Sardar's behest. He spoke of secret meetings between them to plot his downfall.

As Nariman let off steam, the press kept up the attack against Sardar. It continued for weeks and months, deeply wounding Patel's feelings.

Nehru replied to Nariman, expressing surprise at his complaint: 'You are allowing your imagination to carry you away from facts... It surprises me that you...make serious charges without any real basis...'

But Nariman refused to back down.

Meanwhile, Patel said not a word. When a correspondent from *The Tribune* newspaper of Lahore approached him for comments, he only remarked, 'Nariman belongs to a small and sensitive minority of Parsis...' Dignity demanded silence.

Not getting the desired response from Nehru, Nariman shot off angry letters to Gandhi and to the press, making numerous allegations against Patel. More newspapers jumped on the bandwagon, publishing what they termed as *conclusive proof* against Patel, who was being painted as an unfeeling destroyer of political careers. The relentless propaganda seemed to have no end.

'Don't lose patience,' Gandhi advised Patel, urging him to issue a statement about the matter.

Patel knew Nariman – they had spent some time together during the Bardoli Satyagraha in Gujarat, and he too was an ardent nationalist and a Gandhian. At Gandhi's behest, Sardar, who had stayed studiously silent thus far, issued a brief public response at Wardha. 'I have never, directly or indirectly, influenced this election... I have no personal grudge against him... The suggestion that Nariman was not elected because he belonged to a minority community is false and malicious.'

The statement provoked Nariman; he issued a counter-statement. The matter refused to die down.

'I am prepared to examine all your charges,' Gandhi suggested an enquiry. 'If I feel convinced that you have been unjustly treated by Sardar, I shall unhesitatingly say so. But if you are found to be in the wrong, you should apologize to Sardar.'

Nariman was not prepared to apologize. Instead, he questioned Gandhi's impartiality and asked for protection to be given to all witnesses since, according to him, Patel was powerful.

The two-person committee comprising Gandhi and Advocate General Bahadurji, a Parsi himself, investigated Nariman's allegations. At the hearings, Khurshed Nariman, a fine lawyer, argued his own case. Vallabhbhai Patel chose not to appear, preferring that the evidence speak for itself. After examining all the material, the arbitrators came to the conclusion that 'Sardar Vallabhbhai Patel made no attempt to influence the vote of anyone'.

After the report was shown to Nariman, Gandhi gave him a choice – either he could present the decision before the public, or he could issue a frank statement accepting the findings. Nariman chose the second option and issued a brief statement of regret.

But soon thereafter, he did a somersault. He charged Gandhi with favouritism and demanded that the decision of the arbitrators be examined afresh by Velinkar, a leading lawyer in Bombay. Sardar refused to consult a senior lawyer.

In the end, the Congress Working Committee declared Nariman unworthy of holding a position of trust, and he was asked to leave his city chair.

Ten years after the saga, Khurshed Nariman apologized to Sardar Patel. He also requested that he be permitted to rejoin the Congress. Patel agreed to take him back.

On 4 October 1948, Khurshed Nariman died in Delhi. At the request of his relatives, Sardar Patel arranged for his body to be brought to Bombay on a special plane. Paying the freedom fighter a laudatory tribute, Sardar called him 'The Uncrowned King of Bombay'.

Nariman Point in downtown Mumbai is named after Khurshed Nariman, or Veer Nariman, as he was known.

> Sardar knew how to restrain himself when restraint was needed.
>
> V. SHANKAR, SARDAR'S PRIVATE SECRETARY, IN *MY REMINISCENCES*

28

THE SHOW GOES ON

Do business without bitterness

The relationship between Sardar Vallabhbhai Patel and Subhas Chandra Bose is deeply strained after the death of Patel's brother in 1933. Bose, who had looked after Vithalbhai during his last days in Austria, is claiming that Vithalbhai had bequeathed most of his property to him under his will. Vallabhbhai challenges it, and the matter is finally decided in court. A few years after this face-off, Bose is elected as Congress president in 1938, and the responsibility to organize the Congress session falls upon Sardar Patel.

His eyes fixed on the glimmering water of the River Tapti, where workers were constructing a boat bridge, Patel recollected his conversation with Gandhi some months ago when the name of Subhas Chandra Bose had been put forward as the candidate for the next Congress president. Patel had had apprehensions about Bose, but Gandhi had endorsed the choice.

And here he was now overseeing the arrangements for the Congress session of 1938, which was to be held under the presidentship of Subhas Chandra Bose.

'Sardar, I cannot commend you enough on your choice of this site in Haripura for this year's session,' Ramdas Gulati, the engineer overseeing the project, interrupted his thoughts. 'Not only do we have plenty of open space to plan this well, but with the Mandvi forest nearby, bringing in bamboo and timber for construction has become most convenient.'

Surveying the picturesque location, Sardar smiled. 'All landowners in the area have been very generous in making available nearly 500 acres to us,' he said as he walked along the riverbank inspecting the progress. 'And I thought since there are four railway stations within a radius of 30 miles, it would be convenient for those coming to attend the session.'

'The repair work on all roads leading to the stations is going as per schedule,' an assistant updated him.

'Hmm...' Sardar nodded, his eyes surveying the tractors working to level the ground behind them. Patel had a detailed vision for the venue. Large pandals in the centre for the sessions. Smaller tents for exhibitions along the periphery, where local craftsmen could display their handicrafts. A Swadeshi store at one end to promote handspun khadi. Small cottages on the sloping ground at this end to put up Gandhi, Bose and other Working Committee members, where they could enjoy a beautiful view of the river. Well-laid-out gardens were all around. With the electricity supply being worked out, the venue would be a sight to witness at night when fully lit.

He had also paid close attention to aesthetics. Renowned artist Nandalal Bose had been invited from Santiniketan to decorate the venue. He had planned every element most tastefully to display the best of Indian art and architecture. The entrances were thoughtfully painted – the gate leading to the reception depicted a camel resting after a long journey in the desert; the gates leading to the kitchen depicted a hungry boy eyeing a fruit basket and a cat about to swallow a fish. Local Gujarati artists Ravikshankar Raval and Kanu Desai added a local flavour with their creations.

Patel had also set up water works and sanitary facilities, a printing press and a post office, a hospital and a fire station, as well as a bank and a telephone exchange. Over the next few days, no effort was spared in making the session successful and memorable.

Nearly five hundred well-bred cows were brought in to run a top-class dairy facility. Arrangements for rice, flour and oil were made to run a grand kitchen capable of feeding thousands every day. Facilities were planned for grinding and crushing cereals. Cooks and cleaners, carpenters and blacksmiths, drivers and helpers – hundreds in nearby villages found profitable employment, with over a lakh of rupees being spent as wages that went to local farmers and labourers.

'In memory of my brother,' Patel sat down by a boulder along the riverbank as he surveyed the work with satisfaction, 'we shall call this place Vithalnagar,' he said, gazing at the flowing waters of the Tapti.

Much water had flown under the bridge between him and Bose over the years. After having looked after Vithalbhai during his dying days in Austria, Bose had claimed three-quarters of his estate, saying that Vithalbhai had left a will directing Bose to use the money for the political upliftment of India. But questions about the will and how it was made began to swirl in Patel's mind.

Patel had tried to settle the matter with Bose. But the clash had raged on, ending only in court. Ultimately, the Bombay High Court had ruled in Patel's favour. In the end, Patel had refused to take the money; he put it in a trust to be run in his brother's name. It was not about the money at all; for Patel, it never had been.

Whether he was Congress president or a challenger like Subhas Chandra Bose, Patel would not hold back. As it turned out, in the days to come, a splendid session was held in Haripura. Vithalnagar became a grand village within a village. Tens of thousands attended the session, and the population of the village swelled to nearly two lakhs. There was a sandstorm, a cold wave and much rain. But the structures held firm, and everything went as planned.

'Sardar has built a magnificent town!' Nehru congratulated Patel and his team after a glimpse of the arrangements at Haripura. There was a bus service to transport visitors across the venue, which stretched over a mile from one end to the other. Nearly 2,000 teacher and student volunteers were in attendance, all specially trained to ensure that the venue was always kept clean and functional. Thousands of villagers poured in daily to listen to the leaders and could

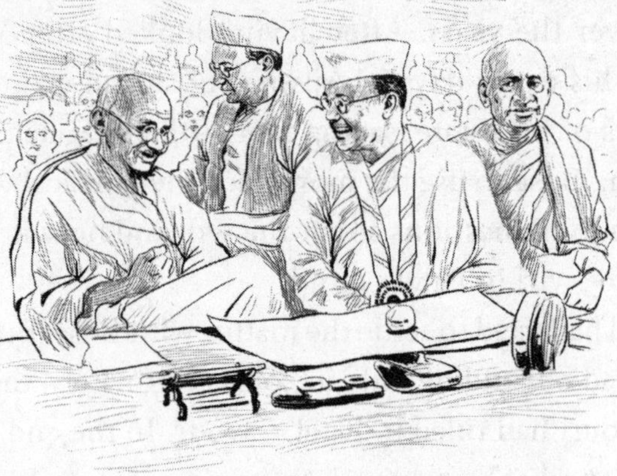

ORGANIZER PAR EXCELLENCE, PATEL PUTS HIS BEST FOOT FORWARD DESPITE PERSONAL DIFFERENCES

eat fresh hot food for just six pice (a unit of currency in pre-Independence India) a meal. Fresh drinking water, clean bathrooms, arrangements for rest, facilities for parking of carts, feeding of bullocks – everything had been carefully thought of and superbly executed.

Regulars who had attended many a Congress session had only words of praise. Despite his stormy interpersonal relations with Bose, Patel had made sure that the show went on and that it went on in great style.

> Sardar was the greatest administrator we had.

ACHARYA KRIPALANI, SENIOR LEADER OF THE INDIAN NATIONAL CONGRESS FROM SINDH

29

FOREVER YOUNG

Keep alive the child within

In 1939, Sardar Patel is living in Bombay with his son Dahyabhai and grandson Bipin. He also has a cottage in Bardoli in Gujarat, where he halts occasionally. He spends his time there tending to fruit trees and flower beds. While there, he also often hosts his friends, including Gandhi.

Once, his friend Narhari Parikh (who would later become Patel's biographer) comes down to Sardar's farmhouse in Bardoli for a holiday with his family, along with some other guests. The house is suddenly chaotic and filled with children, drawing ire from Patel's daughter Mani, who has devoted her life to her father and his work. Committed to the cause, she is often overzealous in safeguarding her father's time and energy. But Patel knows how to have a good time.

FOREVER YOUNG
BARDOLI 1939
ONE SUMMER, PATEL HAD INVITED HIS FRIEND NARHARI PARIKH AND HIS FAMILY, ALONG WITH SOME OTHERS, TO HIS FARMHOUSE FOR A HOLIDAY.
SHU THAYU, VANMALA? WHY IS MY LITTLE FRIEND SO SAD?
IT'S NOTHING...
TELL ME, TELL ME...DID YOUR PAPA SCOLD YOU? IF SO, I'LL TAKE HIM TO TASK. NARHARI...
NO, HE DIDN'T SAY ANYTHING TO US...
THEN, WHY THE GLUM FACES? IT MAKES ME VERY SAD IF MY GUESTS ARE UNHAPPY.
WATCHING PATEL WITH THE CHILDREN OUTSIDE, MANAGER UTTAMCHAND SHAH RECALLED AN INCIDENT.
SOME YEARS AGO, SETH WALCHAND HIRACHAND, THE WEALTHY INDUSTRIALIST, WAS HERE. SARDAR GAVE ME STRICT INSTRUCTIONS TO SERVE THE SETH A SUMPTUOUS LUNCH.

BY CHANCE, GANDHIJI HAPPENED TO BE HERE IN BARDOLI ON THE VERY SAME DAY. AND YOU KNOW PATEL SAHIB...HE INSISTS THAT NOBODY SHOULD BE GIVEN PREFERENTIAL TREATMENT. EVERYONE FROM THE GUESTS TO THE STAFF MUST GET THE SAME FOOD.
SO WHEN BAPU SAT DOWN TO EAT...
...I HAD NO CHOICE BUT TO SERVE HIM SOME JALEBIS.
HEY RAM! THAT MUST HAVE UPSET GANDHIJI. HE INSISTS ON VERY SIMPLE MEALS.
EXACTLY! BAPU SUMMONED ME AFTER LUNCH AND ACCUSED ME OF RUNNING A RESTAURANT!
SO WHAT DID YOU SAY?
'BAPU,' I SAID WITH FOLDED HANDS, 'YOU ARE A GUEST HERE AND SARDAR IS THE HOST. SHOULD I LISTEN TO THE GUEST OR THE HOST?'
AND BAPU LAUGHED IT OFF.
HA-HA-HA-HA
HA-HA
HA-HA

MEANWHILE, IN THE FOYER OUTSIDE, VANMALA HAD FINALLY LET THE CAT OUT OF THE BAG.
MANIBEN SCOLDED US...
WHAT FOR?
WE WERE PLAYING OUTSIDE, AND CAME INTO THE HOUSE ALL MUDDY AND WET.
SO THAT'S WHY YOU STOPPED PLAYING? BECAUSE MY DAUGHTER SCOLDED YOU?
HMM...
ALRIGHT, COME WITH ME.
WHERE?
JUST COME ALONG, KIDS!

JUMP IN! SUMMER'S THE TIME FOR A SWIM.
WHAT? REALLY?
COME ON NOW! ALL OF YOU, IN THE WATER!
CHHAPAAK!
CHHAPAAK!
CHHAPAAK!
CHHAPAAK!

AFTER AN HOUR THEY RETURNED TO THE COTTAGE, DRENCHED IN WATER AND SLATHERED WITH MUD.
NOW, LET'S FORM A TRAIN...
CHHOOK-CHHOOK
MANIBEN, COME HERE. TAKE A LOOK AT YOUR FATHER. ARE YOU GOING TO SCOLD HIM TOO?'

YEARS LATER, WHEN SARDAR WAS UNWELL AND RECOVERING, HE SPENT HIS TIME IN THE JOYFUL COMPANY OF HIS GRANDSON AND HIS FRIEND'S GRANDCHILDREN.
THEY PLAYED, SWAM AND SPENT HOURS LAUGHING OVER 'LAUREL AND HARDY' FILMS.
SPEAKING ABOUT THE DAYS SPENT WITH HIS GRANDPA, HIS GRANDSON BIPIN WOULD LATER SAY, 'WE BANTERED AND JOSTLED AND THREW PILLOWS AT EACH OTHER...
BOOH! BEWARE THE MONSTER!
...UNTIL I REALIZED WHO HE WAS AND GREW DEFERENTIAL'

> Work is undoubtedly worship, but laughter is life.
>
> SARDAR PATEL

CARRYING A LOAD LIGHTLY

Whether he was fighting a battle for freedom or fighting for his own life, Patel's jovial and caring side never left him. Lawyer and freedom fighter K.M. Munshi was a close associate of Patel. Speaking of the time he had spent together with Sardar in jail, when Patel was suffering from severe intestinal pain and was suspected of having rectal cancer some years later, Munshi said, 'In Yerwada Jail, I saw the intensely human side of Sardar's nature. He laughed, cracked jokes, told droll stories. He became our housekeeper, prepared tea for us, looked after our food...' Those with Patel in jail could see his stomach heaving and knew that he was in terrible pain, but Sardar did not speak of it. Even in that state, he wrote letters to friends and colleagues, inquiring about their well-being.

30

THE COMMON TONGUE

Speak to be understood

As a successful barrister, Sardar is a persuasive speaker. He argues forcefully in court, examines witnesses tactfully before judges and makes moving speeches as a political leader. Yet, when he speaks to ordinary people, he uses simple language with visual metaphors, simple proverbs and relatable analogies in the local tongue, making an instant connection.

'There are two kinds of flies. One, the bee that goes far into the jungle and collects honey from flowers; the other type goes and settles on filth and spreads filth. One gives honey to the world, while the other spreads diseases and death. It is the latter type which is at work among you... Do not let such come near you.'

This is how Patel explained the situation to the farmers of Bardoli in Gujarat, who were putting up a historic resistance against the British in 1928. The government was sending out its representatives to convince people to pay higher taxes. Patel, who was leading the Bardoli Satyagraha, used this metaphor, among others, to urge people not to trust members of the government delegation.

This was not the first time Patel was using analogies drawn from daily life to make a deeper point. Speaking to farmers in Kheda some years ago about the oppressive taxation system, he said, 'Remember that a potter puts about a maund (a unit of measuring weight) of things on his donkey. If it is able to carry it, he increases the load to two maunds. Similarly, as you carry the load, the government goes on adding to it. Throw away the load which you have been carrying so far, and do not be afraid.'

Without referring to complex economics and elaborate statistics, through the simple analogy, he conveyed clearly and instantly the point he sought to make.

During these protest movements, farmers felt overwhelmed by the scale of the struggle; they were poor and helpless, while the government was mighty and ruthless. To bolster their resolve, Patel gave them a visual example of a lopsided contest: 'Government has run amok. It thinks it can trample everything under its feet. Even so thinks the mad elephant, priding itself on having trampled even lions and tigers to death, and scorning the little gnat defying him. I am teaching the little gnat today to let the elephant go on in his mad career and then get into his trunk at the opportune moment.'

'Just as the bullock gets frightened at the sound of a car,' he told farmers in Champaran, Bihar, in 1929, 'so you are frightened as soon as any officer of the government or of the zamindar approaches you. Have these men got two heads or four hands? Should they be afraid, or should you? You are the people who give food to the world. The world cannot do without you...much less the zamindar.'

When the government offered measly reforms to pacify irate Indians, Sardar warned people against being tempted with false bait. 'What difference will it make if we replace some foreign officers with Indians?' he thundered. 'Merely by throwing a few drops of Ganga water into the sewage, one can scarcely hope to purify it. There must be a radical change of outlook in the administration.'

When the Second World War broke out in Europe in 1939, the British wanted India's help. *Imagine what would happen to India if Britain were to leave the country in the middle of the chaos,* they asked.

Once again, Patel used a clever metaphor to call out the ridiculous stance of the British government.

'Surely this is a strange question,' Patel said. 'It is as if a watchman were to say to his employer, "What will happen to you if I were to leave you?" The answer will be, "You go your way. Either we shall engage another watchman, or we will learn to keep watch ourselves." But this watchman of ours not only does not go away but also keeps on threatening his employer.'

Proverbs, idioms, analogies, metaphors, stories and jokes – Patel used various devices to persuade and inspire. The point of Patel's communication was not to show off his language but to build connection. 'It is from the speeches of Vallabhbhai in Bardoli that the lovers of

Gujarati discovered how rich their language was,' said his friend and biographer Narhari Parikh.

Even while conveying complex ideas, Patel's style of communication was direct, simple and easy enough for a child to follow. Speaking of her father, his daughter Maniben remarked how Patel always read all the letters written to him and instructed his officers on how they were to reply. If he was not happy with the response drafted by his deputies, he would edit it to make it precise and concise and then tell his assistants, 'People are writing to seek my help. This is not a place for writing long essays to display one's command over English.'

> 'Villagers were moved by the extraordinary eloquence of his speeches and by his astonishingly simple yet effective popular similes and analogies.'
>
> MAHADEV DESAI, FREEDOM FIGHTER AND GANDHI'S PERSONAL SECRETARY, SPEAKING ABOUT PATEL

31

MONEY MATTERS

{ Stay practical, yet principled }

Sardar Patel straddles two contrary worlds. On the one hand, he possesses little and lives a simple, frugal life. On the other hand, as the chief fundraiser of the Congress and its main organizer, he raises and handles a lot of money for party activities. Often, questions about excessive spending are raised by Gandhi and issues about ideology are flagged by Nehru. While Sardar too has ideals of his own, he is a pragmatic man with his feet on the ground.

In 1921, when Patel was placed in charge of organizing the annual Congress session in Ahmedabad, he made innovative changes. For one, he did away with chairs – everyone, including the leaders, was made to sit on the ground. This cut costs and made a strong statement about equality. Secondly, for the sessions, he got tents made of khadi, thus boosting its demand. Water, sanitation, transport, accommodation – everything was meticulously arranged.

Moreover, he paid attention to the smallest of details. Usually, after every session, there was a mad scramble for shoes, which attendees took off before entering the tents. Patel came up with a simple solution: khadi bags for shoes so that everyone could take off their footwear and keep it with them. It not only put an end to the chaos but also increased demand for handspun khadi and generated money as well.

At the conclusion of the event, when the accounts were closed, it was found that, for the very first time, a Congress session had ended up generating a balance for future use, which in turn led to the party finally having funds for building an office in the city. Ever since, Patel acquired the reputation of being a master organizer and fundraiser.

For every event and election thereon, it was Patel who got behind the wheel to keep things running smoothly. In order to raise money, he often turned to industrialists and businessmen like the Birlas and the Dalmias, urging them to play their part in the freedom struggle. 'Come immediately,' he would send a short telegram to Ghanshyam Das Birla every time an urgent need for funds came up. And Birla always obliged.

Gandhi spoke of his philosophy based on trusteeship, under which he believed the wealthy ought to keep their earnings in a trust for the benefit of society and not consume it all themselves. Nehru leaned towards socialist ideals and said, 'What I seek is...cooperation taking the place of competition, and production for consumption and not for profit.'

To Sardar, such ideals were utopian and impractical. Businessmen and industrialists had helped the Congress for years by donating funds. Without their financial support, the Congress party may not have been able to grow and achieve all that it had accomplished. It was one thing to talk of ideals and values, and quite another to survive in the real world. Money kept the party wheels well-oiled and running, and as the man who actually dealt with the cash – distributing funds for election campaigns, organizing programmes and meetings, and paying medical expenses for party workers in need – Patel knew better than most how important that contribution had been.

'Being a farmer myself and having identified myself with the peasantry for years, I know where the shoe pinches,' he had once said, to highlight his differing views.

While Patel knew the value of money, he was also most principled about it. The funds he raised were for the party. He himself possessed next to nothing more than the clothes on his back and was quite clear that those who had dedicated their lives to public service ought to keep things that way.

In fact, when a personal phone call was made from his official residence at Aurangzeb Road in Delhi, a house Patel had been allotted as a minister of the Central government, he would keep a note and ensure it was paid for from his own pocket. When he made calls related to party work – such as calls to the chiefs of the provincial Congress committees – he took care that it was not charged to the government. 'Even Congress funds were not debited for those calls,' recalled Morarji Desai, a Congress leader who went on to become the prime minister of India. Patel's daughter Mani was tasked with keeping account. All those calls were paid out of Sardar's salary.

In 1945, his son Dahyabhai, who lived in Bombay, and his partner had acquired a company in Karachi. However, after Partition, the company became valueless in India. It nearly ruined Dahyabhai, who wanted to exchange the Karachi-based company for land that a Muslim had left behind in Bombay before migrating to Pakistan. To process the paperwork, Dahyabhai came to Delhi.

Patel was incensed. Even the possibility that his son may be seen as seeking or receiving a government favour was enough to anger him. He ordered Dahyabhai to return to Bombay immediately.

When his grandson Bipin visited Sardar after he had a heart attack in 1948, Patel told him, 'As long as I am in this chair, don't visit Delhi...unless I am unwell.' He feared people would contact his family members to reach him for favours, and he did not want to risk their reputation or his own.

Sardar knew the value of money, but not at the cost of his values. Nothing demonstrated his outlook better than a remark made by Gandhi about the matter and Patel's reply to it. Hearing of Patel raising large amounts of money for the party, Gandhi once expressed his disapproval. 'I do not like Sardar collecting money from businessmen,' he told Ghanshyam Das Birla one day.

When Birla conveyed Gandhi's views to Patel, Sardar let out a chuckle. 'That is not Bapu's concern,' he said, shrugging. 'Gandhi's a Mahatma…I am not.'

> When we are faced with thorny problems, and Gandhi's advice is not available, we consider Sardar Patel as our leader.

ACHARYA KRIPALANI, SENIOR CONGRESS LEADER, SPEAKING ABOUT PATEL

32

STANDING FIRM

Place principles over personalities

In 1939, the election of the Congress president turns controversial. Subhas Chandra Bose, who is the sitting president, wants to contest a second term. But the rules of the party provide for a term of only one year. While senior leaders do not think it right for Bose to be made president again, Sardar becomes the face of that opposition.

Congress President Subhas Chandra Bose was riding a wave of popularity. After being elected unopposed at the Congress session in Haripura in 1938, he desired to be party president again.

However, only a few in the party high command agreed. Not Gandhi. Not Nehru. Nor Patel. 'It is only in exceptional circumstances that the same individual is re-elected as president,' said Patel, 'and such circumstances do not exist on this occasion...'

Sardar had several bones to pick with Bose. Despite not liking his election a year ago, he had gone with popular will and even rolled out the red carpet for Bose at the Congress session under his presidentship in Haripura. But Patel was simply not happy with how Bose was running things. On the personal front too, Patel did not see eye to eye with Bose after the unpleasant tussle and court case over his brother Vithalbhai's will.

Yet, even as the opposition mounted, Bose was determined to get another term. With the Second World War looming over Europe, he thought it was the opportune moment to strike, to bring the mighty British to their knees. But instead of pressing down on the pedal when it was time to surge ahead, he believed most Congressmen were taking a moderate stand by considering settling with the government. He just couldn't stomach it. If only he were elected president again, he would steer clear of striking weak bargains and grab the bull by its horns.

However, Patel did not agree with Bose's keenness to exploit England's vulnerability when it was on the back foot against Hitler in Europe. According to Patel, this was not the time to charge but to consolidate. He appealed to Bose not to create a split among Congressmen on the issue and to withdraw his bid to run for party president the second time in a row.

Countering Bose's argument that other leaders would compromise and settle with the British instead of fighting it out, Patel said that the decisions of the party were not determined by the outlook of the president alone but taken jointly by members of the Working Committee.

The disagreements between Bose and Patel were deep. Yet, Patel was opposing Bose's re-election only on the ground of propriety: *Whatever were the rules made for if one was going to throw them to the wind?* Along with some others, he commended Dr Pattabhi Sitaramayya's name to the Congress delegates for election.

Still, confident of success, Bose refused to withdraw. Instead, he countered Sardar. 'In an election contest between two members of the Working Committee,' said Bose, 'one would not expect the other members to take sides in an organized manner.' Bose said he expected members to be free to vote as they wanted.

Contesting the view, Patel pointed out how party elections had taken place in the past, including Bose's own election a year ago, adding that precisely the same process was being adopted this year too.

PATEL AND BOSE – NOT SEEING EYE TO EYE

A war of words followed, and, in the end, neither party stood down. The matter was put to vote. Bose won the election to become party president for the second consecutive time, by a vote of 1580 to 1375.

However, soon thereafter, twelve out of the fifteen Working Committee members of the party resigned. It was also resolved that Bose could not be a member of any elective Congress committee for three years. Dejected, Bose left the Congress, after which he began a new party called the All India Forward Bloc.

For Subhas Bose, his brother Sarat Bose and their followers, Patel continued to be regarded as an opponent.

For Patel, however, it had never been about Bose. As he said, 'For me as for those with whom I have been able to discuss the question, the matter is not one of persons, but of principles.'

> I am prepared to work with the socialist or a capitalist or with a follower of any "ism" but only on one condition that no attempt is made to deceive me. ... Some merely talk; with such persons I shall never be able to get on.

SARDAR PATEL, IN A LETTER TO SOCIALIST LEADER ROHIT MEHTA IN 1934

33

BENDING WITHOUT BREAKING

Let go of rigidity and embrace change

For over twenty years, Patel has been a staunch follower of Gandhi's; some even sarcastically label him Gandhi's 'blind follower'. But in the 1940s, things begin to change. Increasingly, Patel finds himself disagreeing with Gandhi, including on fundamental Gandhian values such as non-violence. While Gandhi sticks firmly to his ideals, unwilling to bend come what may, Patel is more open to accommodating the changing circumstances and taking the practical path.

Gandhi had made his views clear. He did not want independent India to have an army at all. But even as a staunch follower of Gandhi and the principle of ahimsa, Patel couldn't get himself to see things that way. It was one thing for Gandhi to philosophize, quite another for those in charge of running the nation to bear its consequences.

'I am not prepared to declare that in a free India we would have no army,' said Patel.

After all, during the few years of experience that he had had in administering provinces, he had seen firsthand how the military had to be called in on several occasions. Gandhi had not liked it then. He did not like it now. But Patel could not agree.

'We have been following Mahatma Gandhi as faithful soldiers for the past twenty years. We are prepared to do so even now, but Mahatma Gandhi did not want us to follow him blindly...' said Patel candidly. He could not get himself to pretend that he agreed when he did not. Besides, when one was a representative of people, in charge of millions, one couldn't rigidly hold on to personal values.

When India became a free nation in a few years, Patel anticipated troubles of the kind he had seen between different communities. India would need a strong army to maintain peace and keep order, and that strength, he knew, did not come from morals alone. In fact, India went to war with Pakistan in October 1947 – within two months of Independence – after Pakistan launched an attack on Kashmir.

'I feel,' admitted Patel, 'that I would not be able to take my province with me in respect of non-violence to the extent that Mahatma Gandhi expects us to do.'

A debate surrounding this principle had raised its head not far back, as the Second World War had raged on outside India – when the Japanese had been growing stronger, when they had bulldozed Singapore and Rangoon, when they had taken control of the Bay of Bengal. There had been panic in Calcutta, and droves of people had begun leaving the city. One couldn't help wondering – if the Japanese had dared to attack the United States at Pearl Harbor, how long before India fell? The fear of a Japanese invasion had been very real and palpable. And in those circumstances, how would adhering to non-violence protect India?

Over a decade ago, Patel and Gandhi had been imprisoned together in Yerwada Jail. Patel had been preparing a drink of hot water and lime for Gandhi, as he did each morning. When he had been handed the glass one day, Gandhi had covered the steaming hot tumbler of liquid with a piece of cloth.

'What are you doing that for?' Patel had asked Gandhi.

'So that insects don't fall into the hot liquid and die,' Gandhi had replied as he tied the cloth around the glass.

'Come on now,' Patel had said, sighing. 'We cannot practise your non-violence to such limits.'

As he had said then, so he was willing to do now. When principles clashed with survival itself, or when they were being stretched to practically impossible limits, Patel was willing to see them in a new light, be flexible and make room for change.

> 'We have to mellow our idealism or our predilections, by practical considerations.'
>
> SARDAR PATEL, SPEAKING IN DECEMBER 1949 ABOUT LANGUAGE ISSUES

34

ANCHOR DOWN

You can be firm, yet gentle

In 1946, Patel is seventy-one years old. Bogged down by repeated setbacks related to his health and feeling the mounting strain of many responsibilities, he feels the need for a private secretary to assist him. Morarji Desai recommends the name of Vishnu Shankar, a young officer in the Indian Civil Services. Apprehensive about working under a formidable figure like Patel, Shankar nervously appears for an interview before Sardar.

Standing outside the door of the expansive Birla House, Vishnu Shankar checked his watch, then adjusted the silk tie around his neck. *Should he have worn a khadi kurta for this interview instead of a suit? Would Patel hire someone dressed in a suit and tie?* Too late now; the door opened.

'Please wait here,' an orderly led him into a small waiting room. 'I will inform Patel Sahib…'

Shankar dabbed the beads of sweat lining his forehead. Just some days ago, when Sardar had first enquired with his senior, Mr Porter, about hiring him after having received a recommendation from Morarji Desai, Shankar had been in the middle of his preparations to leave for Paris on a foreign mission. Sardar was informed that if approved, it might mark Shankar out for a career in the foreign service. Not wanting to derail the young man's progress, Patel had said, 'In that case I would not like to stand in his way; I'll look for someone else.' But the Paris mission had not worked out as planned, and here he was.

'You may come in now,' said the orderly who ushered Shankar into a spacious drawing room. Sardar was already seated stoically like a senator on an armchair. To his left was his daughter Mani, dressed in a simple white saree. And to his right was Ghanshyam Das Birla, Sardar's friend, to whom the house belonged.

Bowing slightly, Vishnu Shankar entered, feeling the intense gaze of three pairs of eyes on him. 'Namaste.' He folded his hands together.

'Namaste,' Sardar replied, as Shankar took a seat on a low diwan. 'Good morning. How are you?'

'I'm well,' Vishnu Shankar smiled slightly, somewhat uneasy as the trio seated across the room tried to size him up. A bearer came in with some water. And soon, a barrage of questions followed: Where was he from? What was his family background? Where had he worked before? What were his current duties? What did he think of the existing situation in the country? What were his views on the present economic problems?

For nearly two hours, Sardar, Maniben and Birla grilled Shankar on every possible subject. As he reached out for the glass of water before him, Shankar was reminded of the very first interview of his career, with a collector named Mr Brown, and how nervous he had been. But this scrutiny appeared to surpass anything he had ever been through.

'Were you at any point involved in the arrest of Congress workers?' Maniben put across a pointed question, keen to know where Shankar's loyalties lay.

'Fortunately,' sighed Shankar, 'I have never had to send a Congress member to jail during my thirteen years in service. In fact, if I may say so'—he edged forward—'I have great admiration for Pandit Nehru. And my father was associated with Shri Motilal Nehru in the past.'

'Is that so?' Sardar nodded, warming up to the young man.

A few more questions, and Sardar slapped his knees and sprang up. 'I would like you to join as my private secretary as soon as possible.' He extended his hand.

Shankar exhaled in relief as he shook hands with Sardar, feeling as though he had passed the toughest examination of his life. But almost immediately, he was filled with dread. *If the interview had been so gruelling, how much tougher was it going to be to work under such a taskmaster?*

Shankar finished his pending assignments and joined Sardar a week later, filled with apprehension.

'I'm here to sign up for duty,' he told a peon at the door when he arrived at 9.30 a.m. on the first day at Sardar's residence on Aurangzeb Road.

'Sardar is waiting for you in his office.' The peon showed him into the airy circular house encircling an open courtyard. Walking down a long corridor, Shankar went towards Sardar's office room at the south-eastern end. Upon hearing footsteps, Sardar, who was talking to Maniben in the veranda, came into his office.

'Ah! You have come.' He greeted Shankar with open arms.

'Namaste, Sardar.' Shankar grinned sheepishly, not sure how to respond to such an enthusiastic welcome.

'Is this too early for you?'

'No, sir,' replied Shankar. 'I am up at 6 in the morning and ready by 7.30...my grandfather's habits...'

'Is that so? I thought you were like the *gora* sahibs who get up at 8 a.m. and take their tea at leisure,' Sardar chuckled. 'So look – here's the thing. You can have another office room if you want. Otherwise, if you are comfortable, you can work in my room. And whenever you need a break from me or want some solitude or privacy, you can use the veranda or the lawn outside.'

Not having expected such a warm and good-humoured reception, Shankar smiled, his nerves somewhat settling.

'Now...getting to work,' began Sardar as he sank into his chair. 'I would like to read all the reports, Cabinet summaries and important papers myself.' He pointed to the bundles of files in a tray on his desk. 'You should put up the papers before me every day for discussion after going through them. I like to dispose of pending files the very same day.'

'Right,' nodded Shankar, gaining new confidence with every passing minute as Sardar explained precisely what kind of assistance was expected from him.

Later, as the day wound down and Shankar was about to leave for home, Maniben popped her head into the office room. 'Bapuji is calling you for tea.'

'Me?' Shankar narrowed his eyebrows. 'For tea?'

Mani nodded. 'Come...tea is ready.'

Surprised that Sardar should invite to tea a small fry such as him, Shankar went into the drawing room, wondering if he had blundered in some way. Sardar was seated on a sofa, scanning a newspaper.

'There you are.' Sardar lowered the newspaper and looked at Shankar from under his glasses. 'Come...sit.' He beckoned Shankar to pull up a chair beside him. As Maniben brought out tea along with biscuits and savouries, Shankar cracked his knuckles, wondering what this was about. *Why had he been called to have tea with Sardar? What was the matter?*

As it turned out...nothing. They sipped their tea together – Sardar, Mani and Shankar – over which Sardar chatted about a variety of things, asking Shankar's opinion on this or that. Hesitant to share his views before such a senior leader, Shankar spoke little. But sensing his awkwardness, Sardar leaned forward. 'Please don't hold back,' he said. 'I would like you to speak out and speak frankly.'

By the end of the exchange, Shankar couldn't help being struck by the warmth behind Sardar's stern exterior. It amazed him that despite his exalted stature, Sardar was so grounded. His fear and nervousness turned quickly into admiration and joy.

'I never thought him to be so disarmingly kind and considerate and also trusting and accommodating as I found on the very first day…' Shankar would write years later in a book he penned about his days with Patel. 'I remember that as I retired to bed, I felt like a child who had passed a glorious red-letter day – the pleasure was so original, so absorbing and so complete. I looked forward to the next day as a child does to his birthday.'

> We must always behave with the utmost gentleness with people who are our subordinates or inferiors.

SARDAR PATEL, IN A LETTER TO HIS SON WRITTEN FROM JAIL IN 1932

35

ROOM TO DIFFER

Disagreement does not mean disrespect

C. Rajagopalachari, popularly known as Rajaji, is a senior leader of the Congress from Madras province. However, in 1942, he parts ways with the party due to differences of opinion. He eventually rejoins the Congress. When elections are to take place in 1946 for the Central and Provincial Assemblies, leaders in Madras province oppose Rajaji's candidature for being the prime minister (heads of provinces were called prime ministers back then) on account of this background. At that time, Sardar is in charge of the election campaign, and the matter comes up for his consideration.

'Sardar…the issue before Tamil Nadu is simple and clear,' said Muthuranga Mudaliar, a Congress member from Madras Province. 'Rajaji wants to become the prime minister again. And Tamil Nadu does not want him. We have no confidence in his leadership.'

Crossing his arms, Sardar sat back on his seat at Congress House in Bombay, from where he was coordinating the upcoming elections – deciding on candidates, distributing tickets, managing correspondence and allocating funds. There were many issues to attend to across India, and this matter in Madras province was one such.

Over the past few weeks, it had come to light that a group of Congress members was not agreeable to working with Rajaji, ex-prime minister of the province. Rajaji had refused to participate in the Quit India struggle in 1942. And then, of his own accord, he had made a proposal to extend an olive branch to the Muslim League.

Worse, at Rajaji's behest, Gandhi had gone to meet Jinnah fourteen times! None of this had been palatable to Sardar either. But despite his disagreement, he had nothing but regard for the Congress veteran from the south.

'Look, I have no desire to force Rajaji on any of you,' Sardar leaned forward. 'But I will not hide my honest opinion if it is asked for. Especially if, as I hear, my name is being used for propaganda against Rajaji's return to the Congress. Rajaji is one of my dearest friends and lifelong colleagues.' Sardar turned to Sivamurugaswami from Coimbatore. 'It is a black lie to say that I am not willing to allow him into the legislature. I would welcome him back...because I know that he is head and shoulders above all Congressmen in the province in ability, integrity and sincerity.'

Memories of the lifelong association he had spoken of flashed briefly before his eyes. While they now stood divided by differences in opinion and some lows had marred their long association, there was no question at all in Sardar's mind about Rajaji's uprightness.

'You talk of hatred for his leadership...which will perhaps not allow you to appreciate or understand my viewpoint'—Patel interlaced his fingers on the desk—'but we have worked together practically for a lifetime, and we know each other's work.' Patel and Rajaji had differed occasionally on vital matters, but the disagreements, however strong and unpleasant, had not affected their mutual regard, affection and understanding of each other.

Despite his support for Rajaji's return, Patel was also clear about one thing. He could not force his opinion on the leaders of the Madras Congress if they did not wish to be led by Rajaji. Patel was more interested in the future than the past. Yet he felt that 'all our sacrifices would be in vain if we would not absorb talents at our disposal and decide to close our doors against people who have rendered services in the past and made sacrifices more than we have done during our time, simply because on one occasion they differed from us.'

> I have no objection to any honest difference of opinion, but I am a firm enemy of hypocrisy.

SARDAR PATEL, IN A LETTER SOCIALIST LEADER ROHIT MEHTA IN THE 1930S

36

GOAL OVER ROLE

Go beyond the rat race

In 1946, once it becomes clear that Britain would be leaving India soon, the elections to the post of Congress president take on an additional flavour. The person who became party president would also become India's first prime minister on Independence. Patel gets the maximum number of nominations from the Provincial Congress Committees. However, he is asked to step out of the race to make way for Jawaharlal Nehru.

Patel let out a sigh as Acharya Kripalani handed him the note. How fleeting life was: one moment, one is about to be crowned; the very next, the rug is pulled from beneath your feet.

Aware that Gandhi wanted Nehru to be party president, Acharya Kripalani had tried to push it through by getting Nehru nominated even though no Provincial Congress Committee had put forward his name. Patel looked around the room at the members of the All India Congress Working Committee.

Twelve of the fifteen Provincial Congress Committees had nominated him to be the next party president. But he was being asked to step out, to make way for Jawahar – fourteen years his junior – who had not received a single nomination.

Patel nodded. He had done it before, and he would do it again. Without asking a question or raising a protest, he agreed to the request, knowing full well that stepping away now meant that he would not be the prime minister of India.

Of course, he felt disappointed momentarily, but it was not a jolt. At the All India Congress Committee session four years earlier, Gandhi had made his preference for Nehru quite clear. 'Pandit Jawaharlal and I have had differences from the moment we became co-workers,' he said, 'yet I have said for some years and say it now that it is not Rajaji, not Sardar Vallabhbhai, but Jawaharlal who will be my

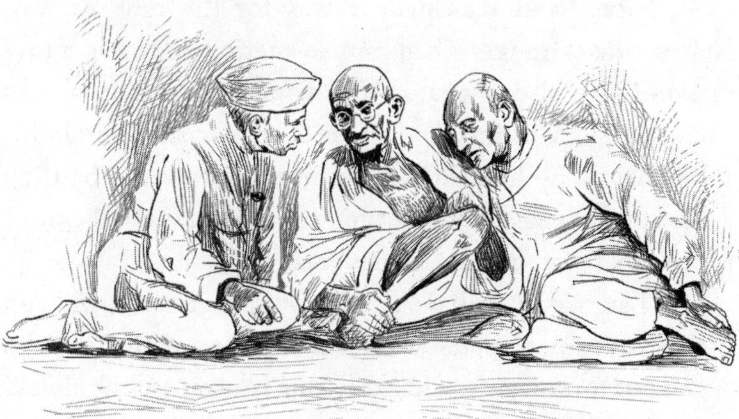

PATEL WITH GANDHI AND NEHRU – THE TOP TIER OF THE CONGRESS PARTY

successor. You cannot divide water by repeatedly striking it with a stick. It is just as difficult to divide us... When I am gone, he will speak my language.'

Sitting beside Gandhi then, as Bapu had spoken those words, Patel had not flinched, for Gandhi had often said that Vallabhbhai was like his younger brother and Jawahar, like his son. And it was not sibling but progeny that was anointed as heir.

With his hands folded, Patel sat down, giving in to Gandhi's will, as he had done before. For this was the man he was. Years ago, he had given up his passage and hard-earned savings to his older brother Vithalbhai so he could fulfil his dreams of studying in England. He had stepped out of the race to make way for Nehru as party president in 1929. Then again in 1937. This was not the first time.

Perhaps, Patel reasoned, it was for the best anyway. Nehru was younger, had more energy and was more dynamic. He also appealed to a wider cross-section – to the youth, to Muslims, and to socialists. Jawahar was in his fifties, while he himself was in his seventies and battling a host of illnesses. A while ago, they had suspected cancer too. Years in jail had made him weak.

'If I had been Jawahar's age, I would have said I will run the government,' Patel would later share with Maulana Azad. But for the moment, exercising restraint, as he always did, he said nothing.

Unknown to Patel, Gandhi had yet another reason for his preference for Nehru. Knowing them better than most, Gandhi had perhaps sensed that Nehru, being ambitious, would have difficulty playing second fiddle. But with Sardar, he was certain, no such problem would arise, because Patel's commitment had nothing to do with rank. As he had remarked to a colleague some years ago, 'Sardar has no parliamentary ambition. He has no ambition for leadership either. Nature has endowed him with certain qualities, and he uses them...'

And just as Gandhi had expected, despite being the popular choice, Sardar displayed no resistance or bitterness in backing Nehru. First in the interim government in 1946, and then in the first government of independent India in 1947, he worked as Nehru's deputy, showing no resentment whatsoever.

Despite Sardar's support and allegiance, there were differences between him and Nehru and disputes too – some of which turned quite bitter, forcing Patel to offer his resignation. But each time, he kept aside his personal feelings and resolved the disagreements on account of the common ground they shared and in the larger interest.

One of their major fallouts came in December 1947, a few short months after India's independence. Patel had decided to assist Nehru from outside while the latter ran the show.

They had ultimately reconciled in deference to Gandhi's last wish that his two most trusted disciples patch up their differences and work together for India's sake.

Nevertheless, Patel's views continued to vary from Nehru's on various matters. Nehru was more inclined towards socialism; Patel was seen as a friend of the capitalists. Nehru was an atheist; Patel had secular values but was a Hindu at heart. They differed on how to handle Kashmir and on the right policy in Hyderabad. They disagreed on China and Tibet. And every time the clash seemed impossible to resolve, Patel agreed to step out of the way.

'If anybody has to go, it should be myself,' he said, while acknowledging Nehru as the leader of the country. 'I have long passed the age of active service. There is, therefore, no question of his quitting office.'

The day before he passed away, lying in bed, he dwelt on several memories with his private secretary Shankar sitting by his bedside. 'Jawaharlal is one of the nicest persons to work with...' was one of the many things he said.

While on his deathbed, Sardar told his colleague C.R. Gadgil, who had come to meet him, 'I am not going to live...make me a promise...' When Gadgil nodded, Patel took his friend's hand in his. 'Whatever your differences with Panditji, do not leave him.'

> He made his choice out of the two courses that come before a man, namely, would he live for his country or for himself? Sardar chose his country.

MAULANA AZAD, SPEAKING ABOUT PATEL AT A PUBLIC MEETING IN 1950

37

WHEN IDEALS CLASH

Sometimes, compromise is the best solution

Till early 1947, Patel is strongly against any proposal to divide India and opposes Jinnah's idea of Pakistan. As independence for India nears and troubles with the Muslim League grow, he becomes the first Congress leader to accept Partition. With League-sponsored communal violence tearing India apart, he reads the writing on the wall; unity is desirable, but not at the cost of peace. Once convinced, he is tasked with persuading the stiffest opponent to Partition – Gandhi.

'Nobody likes the division of India, and my heart is heavy,' said Patel as he delivered a keynote address before a sombre gathering of leaders at the All India Congress Committee in June 1947. 'But the choice is between one division and many divisions. We must face facts. We cannot give way to emotionalism and sentimentality.'

He had arrived at that decision, Patel insisted, not out of fear but to prevent the hard work of many years from going to waste. He had never wanted Partition and had never believed in Jinnah's two-nation theory, which claimed that Hindus and Muslims were meant to live as two separate nations. In every speech Patel had given, he had urged Hindus and Muslims to live together in harmony. But there appeared to be no other practical solution. Riots were raging across Bihar, had devastated Calcutta and killed over 50,000 in Punjab. He would rather they separated as warring brothers and adopted a live-and-let-live policy.

'Freedom is coming...' he stressed on the brighter side. 'We have 75 to 80 per cent of India, which we can make strong with our own genius.'

The nine months that Patel had spent trying to run a part-time government jointly with the Muslim League had left no doubt in him whatsoever. Working together with Jinnah and his party was impossible; they were hell-bent on civil war, on chaos, on disorder. His goal, on the other hand, was India's safety, its stability, its progress. If letting go of a part of the territory could help in achieving the ultimate objective, perhaps it was worth the price. Convinced, he would now need to persuade his mentor. And that was going to be no easy task.

On a hot evening at the end of May, Patel met Gandhi in a little room in Bhangi Colony in Delhi, where Gandhi was staying. Patel had given his word to his colleagues that he would bring Gandhi around, and he was determined to make that happen.

On the evening of 28 May, they spoke for nearly an hour. On the 29th, for an hour and a half. On the morning of the

30th, for nearly two hours. Just them – Gandhi and Patel. 'It is either Partition or civil war,' Patel explained, pointing out the horrific violence in the country. It was painful to agree to Partition; after all, he himself had first dismissed the idea as Jinnah's mad dream. But as things stood now, it would be like having a diseased limb amputated so that the rest of the body could live on in sound health.

Had they not tried their best to make peace with Jinnah and the League? How much more could one bend? How many times had the Congress tried to settle with the League only to have their fingers burnt? Had Gandhi not personally gone to meet Jinnah at his home in Bombay to find an amicable solution? Fourteen times!

Each time, Jinnah had spurred him; each time, he had wanted more; each day, his speeches grew more venomous. If one were to think pragmatically, Partition was in India's best interests.

After listening to Patel for hours, a very pained Gandhi gave in. 'I have not that strength today,' said the frail seventy-seven-year-old, 'or else I would declare rebellion single-handedly.'

Gandhi expressed his anguish: 'Today I find myself all alone,' he lamented. 'Even Sardar and Jawaharlal think that my reading is wrong and peace is sure to return if Partition is agreed upon.' He made it clear that he disagreed with India being broken up but would not stand in the way anymore.

In the end, the matter was put to vote before the All India Congress Committee. One hundred and fifty-seven voted for, 27 voted against, and 32 remained neutral, paving the way for the Partition of India. It was one of the only times ever that a resolution had been approved in total silence.

A few days later, Patel heard of a request from a jubilant Jinnah, who had got what he wanted and now wanted more. 'Mr Jinnah has been pressing for an agreement for India and Pakistan to have joint control of Calcutta for six months,' V.P. Menon, then the viceroy's constitutional adviser, conveyed the message.

Patel looked at him sombrely. A few days earlier, Jinnah had asked for an 800-mile corridor cutting across India to connect East and West Pakistan. The fantastic nonsense Jinnah could come up with infuriated him.

'What shall I say?' asked Menon.

Always swift and decisive, Patel didn't need a moment to think this one over. 'Pakistan wants joint control of Calcutta for six months?' he scoffed. 'Tell Jinnah – not even for six hours!'

> I bear Pakistan no ill-will; I wish them god-speed; let them only leave us to pursue our own salvation and stop meddling with our affairs. ...We only wish to be left alone so that both can live in peace and prosperity, happiness and harmony.

SARDAR PATEL, IN A SPEECH HE MADE IN KATHIAWAR AFTER PARTITION

38

DREAM BIG

{ You can pull off the impossible }

Today, geographically and politically, India is one continuous unit as you see it on the map. But at the dawn of Independence, that unity seems like an impossibility. In July 1947, the subcontinent is a patchwork of about a dozen British provinces and nearly 600 princely kingdoms. The kingdoms are ruled by maharajas and nawabs, who are told that when the British left in August 1947, they could either join India, join Pakistan or remain free. Some of them actually declare independence; some decide to join Pakistan.

At this time, a Department of States is created for the purpose of attempting to unite these states with India. Sardar Patel is appointed the States Minister and V.P. Menon is the Secretary. Bringing the kingdoms all together in fewer than two months seems like an impossibility. But with ingenuity, grit and a never-say-die spirit, Sardar Patel and his team accomplish the monumental feat.

* V.P. Menon – Secretary in the States Department;
C.C. Desai – Additional Secretary in the States Department

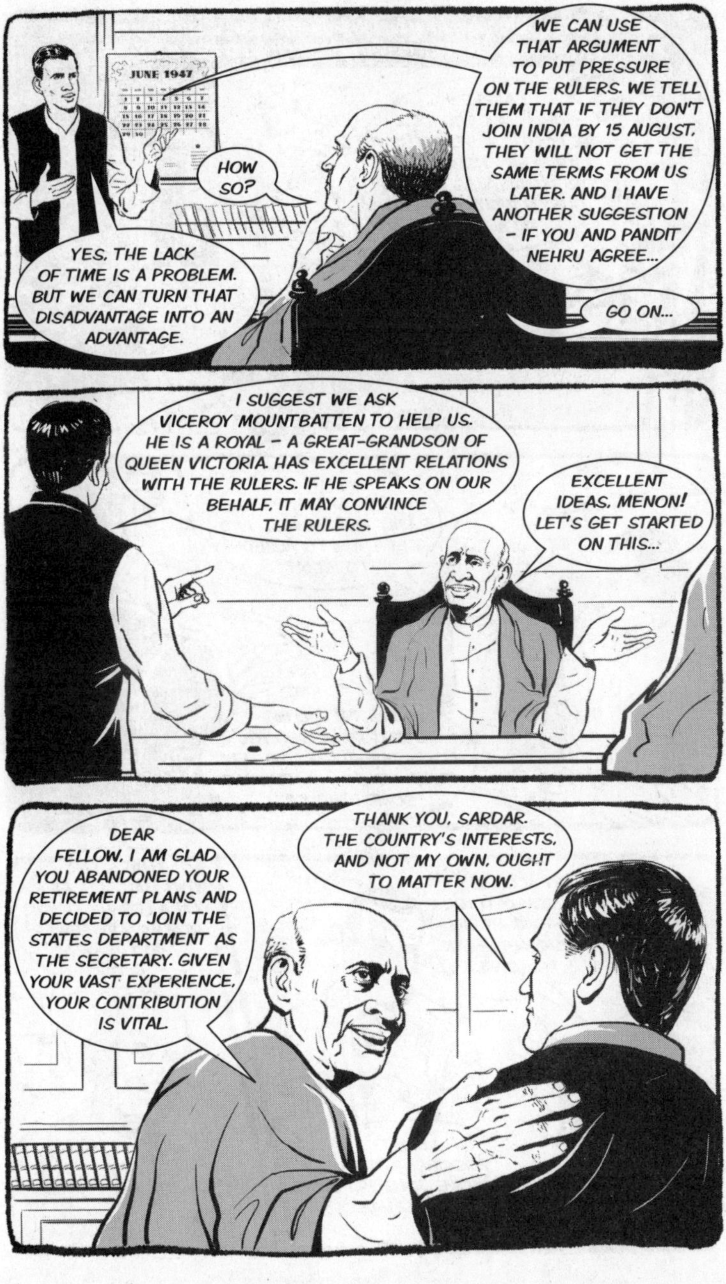
JUNE 1947
YES, THE LACK OF TIME IS A PROBLEM. BUT WE CAN TURN THAT DISADVANTAGE INTO AN ADVANTAGE.
HOW SO?
WE CAN USE THAT ARGUMENT TO PUT PRESSURE ON THE RULERS. WE TELL THEM THAT IF THEY DON'T JOIN INDIA BY 15 AUGUST, THEY WILL NOT GET THE SAME TERMS FROM US LATER. AND I HAVE ANOTHER SUGGESTION – IF YOU AND PANDIT NEHRU AGREE...
GO ON...
I SUGGEST WE ASK VICEROY MOUNTBATTEN TO HELP US. HE IS A ROYAL – A GREAT-GRANDSON OF QUEEN VICTORIA. HAS EXCELLENT RELATIONS WITH THE RULERS. IF HE SPEAKS ON OUR BEHALF, IT MAY CONVINCE THE RULERS.
EXCELLENT IDEAS, MENON! LET'S GET STARTED ON THIS...
DEAR FELLOW, I AM GLAD YOU ABANDONED YOUR RETIREMENT PLANS AND DECIDED TO JOIN THE STATES DEPARTMENT AS THE SECRETARY. GIVEN YOUR VAST EXPERIENCE, YOUR CONTRIBUTION IS VITAL.
THANK YOU, SARDAR. THE COUNTRY'S INTERESTS, AND NOT MY OWN, OUGHT TO MATTER NOW.

SARDAR PATEL AND JAWAHARLAL NEHRU MET NEARLY EVERY DAY FOR A WALK, DURING WHICH THEY PRIVATELY DISCUSSED KEY MATTERS.
I AGREE – THIS IS A GOOD IDEA. THE POLITICAL DEPARTMENT HAS BEEN ENCOURAGING THE MAHARAJAS TO KEEP OUT OF INDIA. WE NEED TO ACT FAST.
WILL YOU HELP US SPEAK TO THE RAJAS AND NAWABS AND GET THEM TO ACCEDE TO INDIA?
WELL, I'M WILLING TO HELP. PROVIDED YOU ALLOW THE RULERS TO KEEP THEIR TITLES, PALACES AND SOME PRIVILEGES.
I ACCEPT – PROVIDED YOU BRING ME ALL 565 APPLES IN THE BASKET.
I CAN'T POSSIBLY BRING IN EVERYONE. WHAT IF I BRING YOU A DOZEN LESS?
THAT'S FAR TOO MANY. I'LL GIVE YOU A LEEWAY OF SIX STATES. ANY FEWER AND THE DEAL IS OFF.

MEANWHILE, A FEW STREETS AWAY IN DELHI...
MOHAMMAD ALI JINNAH, HEAD OF THE MUSLIM LEAGUE HAD INVITED MAHARAJA HANWANT SINGH OF JODHPUR FOR A MEETING.
IF JODHPUR JOINS PAKISTAN, I'LL GIVE YOU WHATEVER YOU WANT. INDIA WILL NEVER BE ABLE TO GIVE YOU A BETTER DEAL.
HERE – I'M GIVING YOU A SIGNED BLANK CHEQUE. PUT IN WHATEVER CONDITIONS YOU WANT...
I...UH...I'M VERY GRATEFUL...BUT, UH...I WILL NEED TO CONSULT MY MINISTERS AND GET BACK TO YOU.
SARDAR, I JUST HEARD THAT JINNAH MET THE MAHARAJA OF JODHPUR AND JAISALMER. HE OFFERED THEM MANY PERKS IF THEY JOIN PAKISTAN.
WE JUST HEARD THAT MUSLIM LEAGUE LEADER LIAQAT ALI KHAN MET THE NAWAB OF RAMPUR ASKING THAT RAMPUR TOO JOIN PAKISTAN.
BUT RAMPUR IS DEEP INSIDE INDIA!

SO IS BHOPAL... AS IS HYDERABAD. THAT HASN'T STOPPED JINNAH FROM APPROACHING THEM. IF WE DON'T DO SOMETHING ABOUT THIS, THESE STATES WILL BE LIKE A CANCER IN INDIA'S BELLY.
JINNAH EVEN DREAMS OF GETTING AN 800-MILE CORRIDOR ACROSS INDIA TO CONNECT WEST AND EAST PAKISTAN!
MAHARAJA HANWANT SINGH OF JODHPUR IS A YOUNG FELLOW IN HIS 20S, WHO HAS JUST LOST HIS FATHER. JINNAH IS TAKING ADVANTAGE OF HIS INEXPERIENCE.
SARDAR... THE MAHARANI OF TRIPURA HAS ALSO WRITTEN TO US.
THE MAHARAJA OF TRIPURA PASSED AWAY A FEW WEEKS AGO, AND THE PRINCE IS A YOUNG BOY. THE MUSLIM LEAGUE IS CREATING TROUBLE THERE TOO.
THE LEAGUE IS TRYING TO ORCHESTRATE A PALACE COUP BY PLACING THE MAHARAJA'S YOUNGER BROTHER ON THE THRONE. THEY WILL GET HIM THE THRONE AND HE WILL MAKE TRIPURA JOIN PAKISTAN.
AND JUNAGADH - HAS THE NAWAB CONVEYED HIS DECISION YET?

OVER THE NEXT FEW DAYS, SARDAR ISSUED A STRONG STATEMENT, APPEALING TO RAJAS AND NAWABS TO DO THE RIGHT THING FOR INDIA'S FUTURE. HE MET RULERS, TRAVELLED EXTENSIVELY AND NEGOTIATED TERMS.

IN ABOUT A MONTH, MOST OF THE 565 PRINCELY STATES HAD JOINED INDIA. EVEN POWERFUL DYNASTIES SUCH AS THE GUPTAS AND THE MUGHALS HAD NOT UNITED INDIA INTO ONE, AS SARDAR PATEL AND V.P. MENON MANAGED TO DO IN RECORD TIME. FOR THE FIRST TIME IN HISTORY, THE WHOLE OF INDIA WAS INTEGRATED AS ONE.

OVER THE NEXT YEAR, SARDAR WENT FURTHER.
HE MERGED KINGDOMS, MODERNIZED THEIR ADMINISTRATION AND USHERED IN DEMOCRATIC REFORMS.
INDIA
ALL ARTIFICIAL BARRIERS BETWEEN DIFFERENT PARTS OF INDIA WERE BROKEN DOWN TO INTEGRATE IT INTO ONE UNIT.
IT WAS AN UNPARALLELED ACHIEVEMENT.
MOHIT SUNEJA / 2025

A FEW YEARS LATER, SARDAR WAS ON A TOUR OF KERALA...
SHANKAR, DO YOU REALIZE WHERE YOU ARE?
YES – AT KANYAKUMARI, THE CONFLUENCE OF THE ARABIAN SEA AND BAY OF BENGAL WITH THE INDIAN OCEAN.
YOU ARE AT THE FEET OF MOTHER INDIA! CLOSE YOUR EYES AND CONTEMPLATE WHAT LIES BEYOND THIS POINT UP TO THE HIMALAYAS, AND HOW ALL THAT HAS BEEN WOVEN INTO ONE GREAT EXTENSIVE FABRIC.
FOR BRINGING TOGETHER AND INTEGRATING HUNDREDS OF KINGDOMS INTO THE INDIA THAT WE NOW HAVE, SARDAR PATEL'S BIRTH ANNIVERSARY (31 OCTOBER) IS CELEBRATED AS NATIONAL UNITY DAY OR 'RASHTRIYA EKTA DIWAS'.

> The problem of the princely states is so difficult that you alone can solve it.

GANDHI TO PATEL, JUNE 1947

MAKING THE IMPOSSIBLE POSSIBLE

When the British decided to leave India in early 1947, nearly half the Indian subcontinent comprised territories ruled by rajas and nawabs (called the princely states). These rulers were informed that after the British left, they were free to join India, join Pakistan or remain free.

Some states like Travancore and Hyderabad declared independence. There was apprehension that many of the other 565-odd kingdoms would do the same. Some rulers began negotiating terms with Jinnah to join Pakistan. Junagadh (in Gujarat) actually did. Meanwhile, the Nawab of Bhopal tried to get the princes to form a third nation called Princestan.

Averting all these challenges, the unification of India under Sardar Patel's leadership was such a feat that it prompted Soviet Premier Nikita Khrushchev to remark, 'You Indians are amazing people! How on earth did you manage to liquidate the princely states without liquidating the princes?'

39

NO PLACE FOR YES-MEN

Seek challengers, not cheerleaders

Before Independence, the administrative units of the country are not based on language grounds (such as the states today). For example, the province of Madras comprised areas with speakers of Tamil and Telugu, among other languages; the province of Bombay included regions that spoke Marathi, Gujarati and Kannada as well as other languages. After Independence, there was a demand for redrawing the internal map based on language. As home minister, it is a matter Sardar Patel must consider, along with Home Secretary H.V.R. Iengar.

Home Secretary H.V.R. Iengar found himself in a peculiar situation as he entered the office of Home Minister Vallabhbhai Patel for the meeting.

A few days ago, the Congress Working Committee had made a decision. Giving in to the demand for reorganizing the states of independent India on the basis of language, it had decided that immediate steps should be taken for the formation of the state of Andhra for Telugu-speaking people.

However, Iengar had grave misgivings about the proposal. Religious differences had torn the country apart, and relations between Hindus, Muslims and Sikhs had barely simmered down. If state boundaries were now to be redrawn based on language, it would open up yet another Pandora's box of division and conflict. But how was he to tell Patel that he disagreed, when Patel had been part of the Congress Working Committee that had approved the proposal?

Sensing his unease during the discussion, Patel asked him about it openly. 'You seem edgy, Iengar. What is the matter?'

'Sir…I…uh…' Iengar shifted in his seat.

'The very first day that we began working together, I told you…and in fact all the other secretaries as well… that I expect you to share your honest opinions with me,' said Patel, 'even if they do not align with my views… is it not?'

Iengar nodded slightly.

'Your job is to challenge me, to give me inputs to make the right decision. Not to fear me and praise me. If you do not give your honest opinion…then please, you better go.'

'Sir'—Iengar cleared his throat to explain his predicament—'the Congress Working Committee resolution has been passed by Pandit Nehru, Maulana Azad, Rajendra Prasad and you – all of you Cabinet ministers,' he mumbled. 'How can *I* say anything about it?'

Interlacing his fingers on the table before him, Patel leaned forward. 'Are you or are you not the home secretary to the Government of India?'

'Of course I am, sir,' replied Iengar, taken aback.

'Then...do your duty as the home secretary. What is your honest view about the proposal to create states based on language grounds?'

'Sir, I think it will be detrimental to India...' Iengar began hesitantly. 'At this moment, we need to consolidate and come together...this will further divide the people and break up the nation. Forces of disruption will be let loose by this move.'

'If that is your considered view,' said Patel, 'prepare a note for the Cabinet of the Government stating clearly the implications of this policy according to you. It makes no difference who proposed it – it could be Nehru or Azad or Prasad or even me. That should not matter at all. Your job is to analyse the problem fairly and give your frank view.'

'Yes, sir...' Iengar nodded, filled with confidence.

In the end, Iengar prepared a detailed study and placed it before the Cabinet. As a result of his inputs, the proposal to create states on linguistic grounds was put away. Even Patel changed his views, convinced by Iengar's arguments, and said it would retard the gains that India had made so far (states were organised on linguistic grounds after Patel's death, starting with Andhra in 1953). Later, Iengar would joke about it with Patel, pointing out how he had managed to get Home Minister Sardar Patel to overrule Congress Leader Sardar Patel.

Sardar's backing of his home secretary was not a solitary occurrence. It was in line with the confidence he had expressed in the civil services several times over. Just before Independence, Sardar had invited about thirty senior members of the services home. Many of them had feared that the new government of independent India would not trust officials who had once served the British. But that one warm gesture had ended all their fears. Sardar had asked them to forget the past and join him in serving the country in the future, and they had all willingly pledged their services to the nation.

In fact, in 1949, as the Constitution of India was being drafted, Sardar insisted upon having two key provisions inserted into it (Articles 311 and 314) in support of administrative and police staff that would make it difficult for politicians to punish them. 'It is a bad workman who quarrels with his instruments...' he argued. 'Every man wants some sort of encouragement. Nobody wants to put in work when every day he's criticized and ridiculed in public.'

For his role in supporting them, Patel is regarded as the patron saint of the civil services. The day after he died, 1,500 civil officers met in New Delhi to mourn his death, and pledged complete loyalty and unremitting zeal in serving the nation. A gesture like that had never been seen before, nor has it been recorded ever since.

> Sardar Patel never interfered in my work. I did my job in the full knowledge that I had his authority to carry out his policy. He accepted my views on most matters; if he disagreed, he would tell me so. We would then discuss and argue the issue, and if I succeeded in convincing him of the correctness of my view, he would readily accept it. I have never seen him swayed by considerations of prestige.

V.P. MENON, STATES SECRETARY, IN
INTEGRATION OF THE INDIAN STATES

Patel once asked the Law Secretary Shavax A. Lal to give him his opinion on a certain issue. Having had a bad experience after expressing an unfavourable opinion to another minister, Lal held back. 'Would you like to know my honest opinion?' he asked Patel hesitantly.

'Does the Government pay you 4,000 rupees a month for your dishonest opinions?' Patel shot back. 'It is your duty to give your honest opinion. It is then up to me to accept it or not!'

40

ONE NATION, MANY VOICES

Look beyond the narrow lens

In the 1940s, Hindustani is the commonly used language of communication across much of north India. It is a bridge language drawing from both Hindi and Urdu. However, as Partition nears, language becomes a hotly contested issue. When Pakistan adopts Urdu as its national language in 1947, it begins being viewed with hostility among some in India.

In this atmosphere, as minister for Information and Broadcasting, Patel has to decide what language should be used on All India Radio, which is the government's most important mode of communication with the people. In December 1949, he conveys his outlook to the man taking over charge of the ministry from him.

'Diwakar, if I say to you'—Patel edged forward on his chair on a cold December morning—'that the main purpose of communication is to be understood – would you agree or disagree?'

'Hmm...' Ranganath Ramchandra Diwakar nodded in agreement. A veteran leader of the Congress from Karnataka, aside from being a writer, he was now in charge of Information and Broadcasting, a portfolio previously held by Patel.

'If that is indeed the case, what, may I ask, is the point of airing programmes on the radio in literary Hindi, embellished with heavy Sanskrit...that most people are unable to follow?'

'Sardar'—Diwakar tugged at his muffler, conscious of the long tussle between Congress and League supporters over language before Independence—'some groups have voiced their objections over the usage of Urdu in radio programmes, now that Urdu is Pakistan's national language. They insist that we use pure Hindi, along with literary Sanskrit words in place of Hindustani.'

Interlocking his fingers on the desk before him, Sardar leaned forward. Radio was the most powerful medium for dissemination of news and information from the government to the citizens. *What was the point, if most people did not follow what was being said?* 'The language used on the radio must undoubtedly be chaste and dignified,' he clarified. 'But more importantly, it must be understood and appreciated by the common man. And Urdu, like Hindi, does not belong to a single region,' argued Patel. 'There are many in east Punjab, in the United Provinces, in Bihar... and several other places who speak Urdu.'

'I see what you mean'—Diwakar sat back—'but some of our colleagues at All India Radio have strong views about this. I am under pressure from more than one quarter holding quite extreme views on the matter.'

'Diwakar'—Sardar held up his hand—'the protagonists of Hindi have to realize that a national language is formed not by fanaticism, nor is it imposed by statute, but grows consciously and subconsciously by the efflux of time, with the inevitability of gradual recognition. The All India Radio is not, and should never become, a literary club. Once you turn it into a club of that sort, it will become exclusive and cease to be a national institution.'

Diwakar nodded in agreement. Although a professor of English, he knew just as well as anybody else that some of the slogans that had fired up the masses during India's long struggle for Independence had Urdu roots. This included the most popular of them all – 'Inquilab Zindabad' – that heady cry for freedom, coined by Maulana Hasrat Mohani, the Urdu poet who expressed his love for Lord Krishna with as much vigour and devotion as he had for the nation.

'In my opinion,' continued Sardar, 'Urdu must be included as one of the main languages of the All India Radio stations in provinces where it is spoken...particularly if we have to make the radio an effective instrument of promoting the ideals of a secular state among Muslims and refugees.'

'Thank you for conveying your thoughts so clearly, Sardar,' nodded Ranganath Diwakar, aware that Sardar had even approved a plan for an Urdu magazine named *Aajkal.*

'Whoever heads and manages the All India Radio,' said Sardar as he left, 'must be guided by a breadth of vision and outlook...and that vision should go beyond extremism of any sort.'

> Little minds and great responsibilities go ill together.

SARDAR PATEL IN MID-1949, AFTER RECONCILING AN ACRIMONIOUS DEBATE BETWEEN PARTY MEMBERS FROM NORTH AND SOUTH OVER WHETHER HINDI OR ENGLISH SHOULD BE THE NATIONAL LANGUAGE

41

A FRESH START

Everyone deserves a second chance

In 1948, when Patel is the deputy prime minister of independent India, he hears about the sorry plight of Ishwarlal Bhagat, an old acquaintance from his days in the Ahmedabad Municipal Corporation, where Patel learnt the ropes of politics. Back then, Patel had helped Bhagat get the job at the municipality, but instead of being grateful, Bhagat had played a part in Patel's ouster from the municipality. Now, many years later, the tables had turned.

Tossing his shawl over his shoulder, Patel gazed at the sun rising behind the Bada Gumbad at Lodhi Gardens in Delhi, mulling over the news he had just heard.

Old memories surfaced from nearly thirty years ago when he had been a young barrister in Ahmedabad, living a very different life. He recalled the face of Ishwarlal Bhagat, the young man he had helped get a job as municipal secretary in the city's municipality.

As Patel walked briskly down the dirt path towards Athpula, catching up on exercise in the early morning hours before the day's events caught up with him, he recalled how Bhagat, who had been appointed on a temporary basis, had managed to bypass due process and get himself promoted to a higher post even before completing his probation. Patel had opposed this procedural lapse and complained to the municipal commissioner about the illegality of the decision. But Bhagat's indiscipline had continued unchecked.

Pausing at the bridge, Patel recalled the many differences that had arisen between them back in 1919. At one point, Bhagat had to be stopped from issuing any communication under his name. But despite every attempt to keep him in check, Bhagat had managed to make his way around and outmanoeuvre Patel, even getting himself appointed as chief officer in the municipality when Patel was its president.

Ultimately, the man had proved too exhausting for Patel, becoming the cause for Patel's resignation from the corporation. His colleague and friend Ambalal had written to him urgently after that, urging Patel not to treat Bhagat's appointment as a vote against him. A resolution requesting Patel to reconsider his decision was also passed. But Patel's decision was made. Quitting his post, he never returned to municipal politics again.

As thoughts took him back, Patel was reminded of another man with whom he had locked horns in recent years – the brilliant diwan of Travancore, C.P. Ramaswami Iyer, more popularly known as CP. Over the last few years, they had had several collisions, with CP boldly declaring that Travancore would become an independent nation from 15 August 1947 onwards. But much water had flown under that bridge. Forgetting past hostilities, Sardar had made his peace with CP, even invited him home, and recommended him for serving India in an important capacity.

As a magpie-robin tittered above him, Patel snapped out of his thoughts and resumed his walk, his mind returning to the present. Bhagat, he had recently learnt, was in a dire financial situation. He had lost all his earnings in horse racing, including his bungalow in Ahmedabad. It pained him to learn about the man's current state.

Nodding at familiar passers-by as he exited the gate to return home, Patel considered the matter. The Ahmedabad tussle was done and dusted. He was now in a position of power, while Bhagat was in need of help. *How could he let a matter that was dead and buried come in the way?* After all, he had extended the benefit of the doubt to those several people who had fallen foul with him, giving a second chance to Rajaji, to Nariman, to Nawab Hamidullah and to CP.

Returning home, Sardar Patel wrote out a letter to be sent to Bhagat in Ahmedabad. 'Come to Delhi,' he said, shaking off all baggage of the past. 'I will help you find another job.'

A few days later, Patel received a reply. Owing to his poor health, Bhagat said he was not fit enough to travel. Declining the kind offer with sincere thanks, he later told all his friends about Patel's magnanimous gesture and large heart.

> Sardar is a rough diamond in an iron casket.
>
> SAROJINI NAIDU, FREEDOM LEADER AND POET

42

TRUTH WITHOUT TAINT

Follow reason over emotion

On 20 January 1948, a bomb is thrown into the compound of Birla House, where Gandhi is staying. Gandhi survives, but the arrest of Madanlal, the man who hurled the grenade, and the investigation into the case reveal a conspiracy to kill Gandhi. As home minister in charge of Gandhi's security, Sardar orders nearly two dozen uniformed policemen to stand vigil and more plainclothes policemen armed with revolvers to mix into the crowd during the prayer meetings.

Despite these measures, Gandhi is assassinated ten days later on 30 January 1948 by Nathuram Godse, who fires three shots at Gandhi from close range during his prayer meeting. Godse, a member of the Hindu Mahasabha, and his conspirators accused Gandhi of being pro-Muslim and betraying Hindus. The days that follow see Sardar dealing not just with personal grief over having lost his lifelong guide but also shouldering the blame for the security breach. Deciding to step down, he writes out a letter of resignation.

TRUTH WITHOUT TAINT
NEW DELHI 1948
WEEK AFTER GANDHIJI'S ASSASSINATION, IN SARDAR PATEL'S HOME...
HE'S ASKED YOU TO DISPATCH THIS LETTER TO THE PRIME MINISTER'S OFFICE... HE'S ABOUT TO LEAVE FOR THE CABINET MEETING.
WHAT IS IT?
I THOUGHT SARDAR WAS MADE OF STRONGER STUFF!
BAPUJI...
HMM...
SHANKAR IS VERY UPSET ABOUT YOUR DECISION TO RESIGN.

RING UP JAWAHAR AND TELL HIM I'LL BE SLIGHTLY LATE FOR THE MEETING...
THUD!
SO, I HEAR YOU ARE ANGRY WITH ME?
UH...NOT EXACTLY...
COME... SIT DOWN... TELL ME WHAT IS BOTHERING YOU.
ALRIGHT... TO BE HONEST, I DON'T LIKE YOUR SUBMITTING TO THOSE WHO ARE AGAINST YOU.
I AM THE HOME MINISTER. SECURITY IS MY RESPONSIBILITY. DO YOU THINK MY DECISION TO RESIGN IS WRONG?
UNDOUBTEDLY! YOU ENSURED THAT EVERY POSSIBLE PRECAUTION THAT COULD BE TAKEN TO PROTECT BAPU, WAS TAKEN!

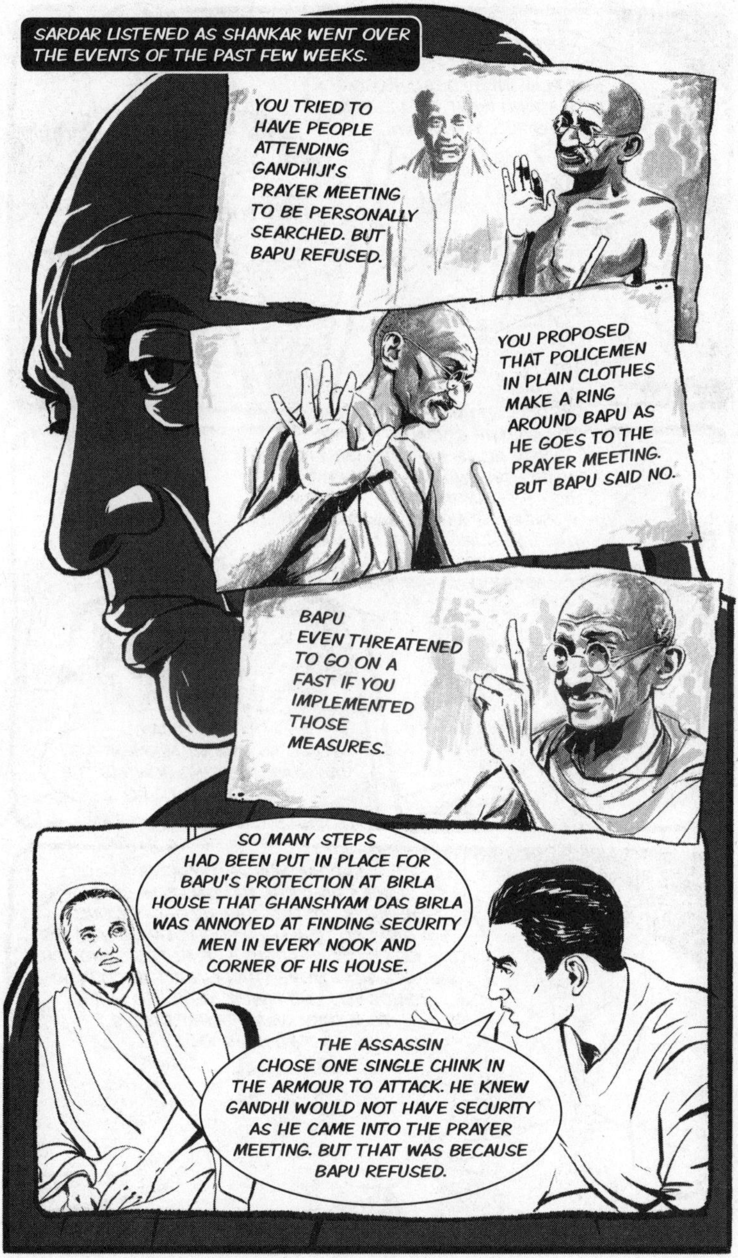
SARDAR LISTENED AS SHANKAR WENT OVER THE EVENTS OF THE PAST FEW WEEKS.
YOU TRIED TO HAVE PEOPLE ATTENDING GANDHIJI'S PRAYER MEETING TO BE PERSONALLY SEARCHED. BUT BAPU REFUSED.
YOU PROPOSED THAT POLICEMEN IN PLAIN CLOTHES MAKE A RING AROUND BAPU AS HE GOES TO THE PRAYER MEETING. BUT BAPU SAID NO.
BAPU EVEN THREATENED TO GO ON A FAST IF YOU IMPLEMENTED THOSE MEASURES.
SO MANY STEPS HAD BEEN PUT IN PLACE FOR BAPU'S PROTECTION AT BIRLA HOUSE THAT GHANSHYAM DAS BIRLA WAS ANNOYED AT FINDING SECURITY MEN IN EVERY NOOK AND CORNER OF HIS HOUSE.
THE ASSASSIN CHOSE ONE SINGLE CHINK IN THE ARMOUR TO ATTACK. HE KNEW GANDHI WOULD NOT HAVE SECURITY AS HE CAME INTO THE PRAYER MEETING. BUT THAT WAS BECAUSE BAPU REFUSED.

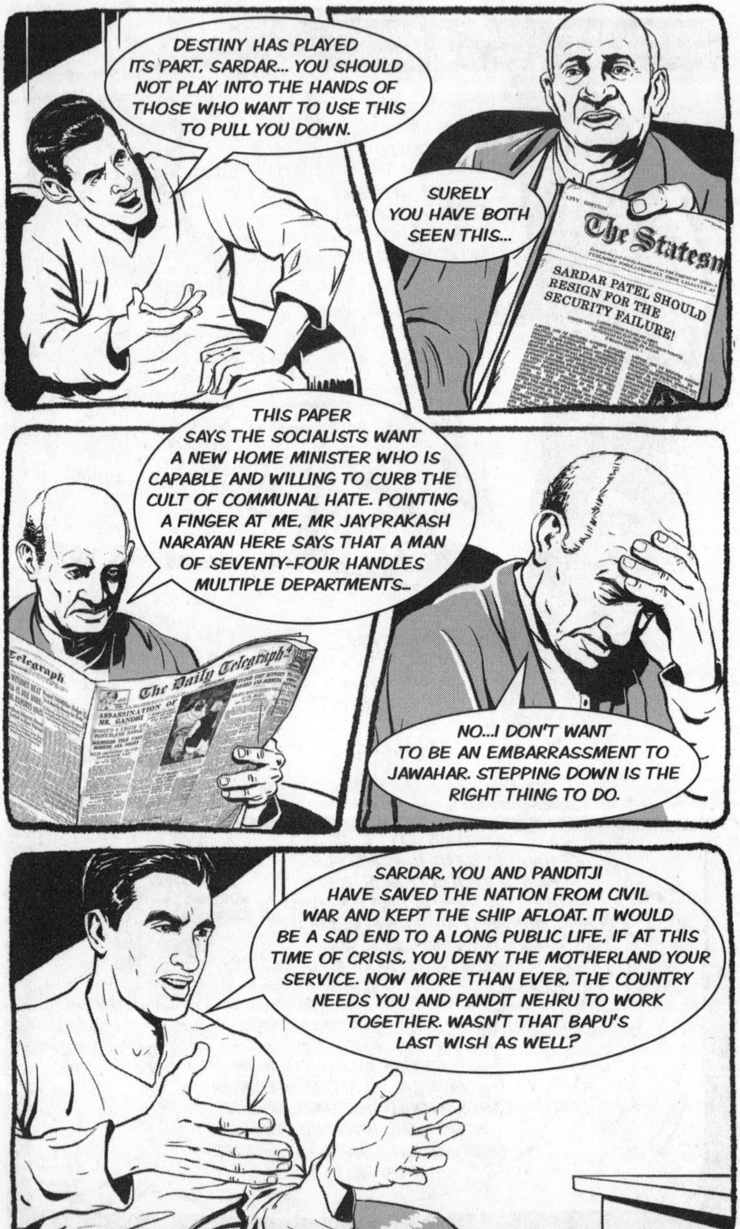
DESTINY HAS PLAYED ITS PART, SARDAR... YOU SHOULD NOT PLAY INTO THE HANDS OF THOSE WHO WANT TO USE THIS TO PULL YOU DOWN.
SURELY YOU HAVE BOTH SEEN THIS...
The Statesm
SARDAR PATEL SHOULD RESIGN FOR THE SECURITY FAILURE!
THIS PAPER SAYS THE SOCIALISTS WANT A NEW HOME MINISTER WHO IS CAPABLE AND WILLING TO CURB THE CULT OF COMMUNAL HATE. POINTING A FINGER AT ME, MR JAYPRAKASH NARAYAN HERE SAYS THAT A MAN OF SEVENTY-FOUR HANDLES MULTIPLE DEPARTMENTS...
The Daily Telegraph
ASSASSINATION OF MR. GANDHI
NO...I DON'T WANT TO BE AN EMBARRASSMENT TO JAWAHAR. STEPPING DOWN IS THE RIGHT THING TO DO.
SARDAR, YOU AND PANDITJI HAVE SAVED THE NATION FROM CIVIL WAR AND KEPT THE SHIP AFLOAT. IT WOULD BE A SAD END TO A LONG PUBLIC LIFE, IF AT THIS TIME OF CRISIS, YOU DENY THE MOTHERLAND YOUR SERVICE. NOW MORE THAN EVER, THE COUNTRY NEEDS YOU AND PANDIT NEHRU TO WORK TOGETHER. WASN'T THAT BAPU'S LAST WISH AS WELL?

PATEL RECALLED HIS LAST MEETING WITH GANDHI ON THE EVENING OF 30 JANUARY, JUST MOMENTS BEFORE A BULLET HAD TAKEN HIS LIFE.
I WANT YOU AND JAWAHAR TO SORT OUT YOUR DIFFERENCES. THE NATION NEEDS THE BOTH OF YOU TO WORK TOGETHER.
I DON'T KNOW WHAT JAWAHAR THINKS ABOUT THE MATTER...
TORN BY GRIEF AND GUILT, NOW MORE THAN EVER, SARDAR MISSED THE VOICE OF THE MAHATMA WHO HAD GUIDED HIM THROUGH EVERY UNCERTAINTY. SO DEEP WAS THE PAIN THAT FIVE WEEKS LATER PATEL WOULD SUFFER A MASSIVE HEART
UNKNOWN TO SARDAR, A FEW BLOCKS AWAY, PRIME MINISTER NEHRU WAS PENNING A LETTER TO HIM.
I AM GREATLY DISTRESSED BY THE RUMOURS ABOUT THE TWO OF US THAT HAVE MAGNIFIED OUT OF ALL PROPORTION ANY DIFFERENCES WE MAY HAVE. WE MUST PUT AN END TO THIS MISCHIEF...
Nothing can lessen my affection and regard for you. We must face the current crisis together as friends and colleagues.
Jawaharlal
SARDAR, THE COUNTRY HAD NOT YET BEEN TOLD THE WHOLE STORY. I CAN COUNTER ALL THESE ALLEGATIONS. WE CAN PUT OUT A STATEMENT IN THE HOUSE IN REPLY TO A SHORT-NOTICE QUESTION.

ALRIGHT... DON'T SEND THE RESIGNATION LETTER. TEAR IT UP AND THROW IT AWAY.
RESIGNATION
STOPPED BY HIS PRIVATE SECRETARY AND SUPPORTED BY THE PRIME MINISTER, SOMEWHAT COMFORTED, SARDAR THEN WENT ON TO DEAL OPENLY WITH THE CHARGE AGAINST HIM.
THIS WAS A CALAMITOUS MISFORTUNE WHICH COULD NOT BE GUARDED AGAINST.
THOUGH OVERWHELMED WITH GRIEF AND GUILT, LOVE AND LOSS, SARDAR LET OBJECTIVITY, AND NOT EMOTION, TRIUMPH IN THE END.

> We must face facts. We cannot give way to emotionalism and sentimentality.

SARDAR PATEL, AT THE AICC MEETING OF JUNE 1947

A BROKEN HEART

Just five weeks after the assassination of Gandhi, Patel's own life was about to end. Just as he sat down for lunch on 5 March 1947, he felt a sharp pain in his chest and placed his right hand over his heart. Those by his side noticed his discomfort and swung into action. It came to light that Sardar had suffered a heart attack. When he recovered consciousness somewhat, Patel wept and mumbled, 'I had to go with Bapu. He has gone alone.'

After he had stabilized the following day, he told Dr Nayar, who had saved his life, 'If Bapu knew, he would scold you. I was on my way to be with him and you stopped me. Everyone says... that I did not take enough care.' He often blamed himself for Gandhi's assassination and told his doctors that the heart attack had been caused not just by the enormous work pressure but also by the heavy blow of Bapu's death.

43

UNAPOLOGETICALLY LIGHT

Don't take yourself too seriously

In 1948, Sardar Patel suffers a massive heart attack and is advised to shift temporarily to the hill station of Dehradun. His daughter Mani, who is his primary caregiver and assistant, is also with him. As he recovers, he begins to receive guests. One of the many people who go to meet Sardar in Dehradun is Mahavir Tyagi, local leader and fellow follower of Gandhiji.

Embracing Sardar warmly, Mahavir Tyagi settled into an armchair in the lobby of the Circuit House at Dehradun, across from Dr Sushila Nayyar, who had been looking after Sardar through his ill health.

'The cool mountain air seems to have done you much good,' smiled Tyagi. 'You seem to be recovering well. Distance from Delhi has helped.'

'Calls and files from Delhi are never too far…' sighed Maniben, Sardar's daughter, as she brought out a tray of tea, gesturing at the stash of files piling up on the corner table for her father's attention.

As Mani put down the tray, Tyagi's eyes fell upon her dull white sari. Pointing to a big patch of cloth covering a torn portion in it, he turned to Sardar. 'Maniben is the daughter of a great man who has united the entire country,' he remarked, referring to the stellar job Sardar had pulled off in bringing together over 500 princely states – big and small – across the length and breadth of the subcontinent to join India. 'Neither Rama nor Krishna nor Asoka nor Akbar...not even the British managed to pull off such a feat of uniting the country that Sardar Patel has managed,' said Tyagi admiringly, for indeed the unification was an unparalleled achievement. 'As the daughter of such a great man – the Sardar of even the rajas and maharajas – surely it is shameful that Mani should be dressed in this sort of a sari.'

Mani smiled slightly. Over two decades ago, as a young seventeen-year-old, she had, of her own will and accord, bundled up all the jewels she had owned – a pair of gold bangles given by her aunt Dahiba, a gold wristwatch gifted by her uncle Vithalbhai after his return from England, a pair of earrings and four other bangles – and donated them all at Gandhi's ashram, pooling them in the cause of India's freedom struggle. Not as a teenager then, much less in her middle age now, did she care about dressing up and wearing fancy clothes.

'Well, she is a poor man's daughter,' Patel shrugged smilingly. 'How can she afford to have good clothes? Her father doesn't make money!'

'Tyagi-ji,' interjected Dr Sushila Nayyar, a tad uneasy at the remark, 'Mani spends the whole day looking after Sardar, attending to his health, answering his calls, fixing his appointments. When she finds some spare time, she spins on the *charkha*, stitches her father's clothes and writes her diary.'

Tyagi nodded. All of that, he knew, was undoubtedly true. After Sardar had fallen ill at the end of the Bardoli Satyagraha in 1928, someone had suggested that he get secretarial help. 'Why not me?' his daughter had volunteered. Ever since, she had doggedly managed his affairs, even after Sardar had hired Shankar as a personal secretary in recent years. She even slept by the telephone to take calls Sardar received at odd hours so that her father's sleep was not disturbed. 'That may be so'—Tyagi put down his cup of tea, turning to Mani with a teasing grin—'but if you happen to go around Dehradun like this, people will take you for a beggar and offer you money.'

Three decades ago, Sardar had been a wealthy barrister, one of the most successful in Ahmedabad, living in a two-storey house with six bedrooms in the heart of the city. He wore crisp, rich suits, fashionable silk ties and polished black shoes, got his collars starched and laundered in Bombay, and smoked expensive cigars. It was said no lawyer in Ahmedabad charged a fee as high as he did. But having given up that attire and appearance for a simple and frugal life, he did not look back with any regret or remorse, even when taunted and teased. Appearances had stopped mattering to him many years ago, when, inspired by Gandhi, he had tossed all his European clothes into a bonfire.

DECIDING TO DEVOTE HIS LIFE FOR THE NATION,
PATEL CONSIGNS HIS WESTERN GARMENTS TO FLAMES

Taking no offence at all at Tyagi's statement, Patel burst into loud laughter. 'The bazaar must be full of people at this time,' he tittered light-heartedly. 'If Mani goes now, by evening she will be able to collect a good amount.'

> Anyone wanting to serve the public needs a thick skin and the ability to swallow both respect and disrespect.

SARDAR PATEL, IN A LETTER TO HIS DAUGHTER MANIBEN IN 1925

44

EMPATHY FIRST

Busy hands, open heart

From the 1920s, Sardar Patel found himself in a leadership position. Heading satyagraha movements to engaging in Congress party work, and from helming government ministries to serving on committees and councils, he was one of the most important and influential leaders of the time. Yet, he was never too busy to notice those in pain or attend to those in trouble and was quick to offer help, often even before he was asked.

'Sardar Sahib has no time.' Shankar appeared at the gate with folded hands. 'I'm sorry he can't see you today.'

Thakur Jaswant Singh turned to the *jagirdar*s from Bikaner who had accompanied him to meet Patel. It had been weeks since they had come to Delhi, weeks of trying to meet Sardar to resolve a matter of vital importance to them. But all their attempts to approach Sardar had been stalled and scuttled.

'I suspect the ministry in Rajasthan has poisoned their ears against us,' said one of the thakurs as they turned to leave. 'Nothing else can explain why Shankar and his daughter Maniben are blocking our access to Sardar.'

'Jaswant-ji,' said another member of the delegation, 'you are a member of the Constituent Assembly. Why don't you approach Sardar when the assembly meets tomorrow?'

Thakur Jaswant Singh let out a sigh. Sardar was a senior leader, attending to dozens of important matters and participating in a number of committees drafting the Constitution in the Assembly. The thought of walking up to him to discuss a local problem felt intimidating. But given that they had made no headway in weeks, that appeared to be the best chance. 'I'll try,' he nodded.

The next day, Thakur Jaswant Singh went early to the assembly and waited in the lobby. As soon as he spotted Patel entering with Shankar, he walked briskly towards them.

'For some days Sardar Sahib will have no time...' said Shankar, moving in hurriedly before Jaswant Singh could say a word to Sardar.

Jaswant Singh stared at Shankar for a moment but pursued Patel nevertheless. 'Please, Sardar...' he called out, 'we have come from Bikaner to Delhi and have been trying to meet you for weeks.'

Stopping as he was about to disappear into a corridor, Sardar turned. 'Give them an appointment for tomorrow,' he told Shankar.

'Sardar...your day tomorrow is completely blocked,' said Shankar.

'Don't worry...' Sardar placed an empathic hand on Jaswant Singh's shoulders. 'I will meet you tomorrow.'

Relieved, Jaswant Singh said a silent prayer. Finally, after waiting for days, they had got the much-desired appointment. The following day, taking along the deputation of the chiefs of Bikaner, Jaswant Singh arrived at Sardar's residence at 3 p.m.

'Sardar is not keeping very well,' Shankar told them as he ushered them into Sardar's office room. 'You cannot take more than fifteen minutes.'

Grateful for the time, the thakurs quickly settled down and were just about to begin talking to Patel, when Maniben cut in. 'I heard some news about many atrocities being committed by landowners in Bikaner...'

Jaswant Singh watched anxiously as the clock ticked away and Maniben went on and on.

'Your time is up,' Shankar said after fifteen minutes. 'Sardar has a doctor's appointment now.'

Dumbfounded, Jaswant Singh exchanged glances with the thakurs. They had not managed to get in a word.

'Never mind the doctor...' Sardar shook his head. 'All that can wait,' he said to them reassuringly. 'You have not told me what you want. Take your time. Explain your problem.'

Over the next hour, Sardar gave the delegation members a patient ear. A few days later, their issue was resolved.

This was not the first time Sardar had been generous with his time and attention. Whether in jail or during a crisis, it was his nature to be accommodating.

During the campaign in Bardoli, a volunteer named Chhotubhai Desai, who had been walking barefoot from village to village, had developed a swelling in his foot. Noticing one morning that Chhotubhai could barely stand, Patel immediately arranged for him to be taken to Harkishandas Hospital in Bombay. When Chhotubhai arrived at the hospital, he was told that had he come half an hour later, it may have been too late.

Throughout his career, as the master organizer and fund manager of the Congress party, Patel had taken care of party workers. If anyone required medical help, Sardar would send them money even before they approached him. If a volunteer was injured, a personally pained Patel would dispatch help at the earliest. When he heard that bureaucratic delays were holding up the transport of suffering refugees during Partition, he intervened by getting Railway Minister John Mathai to cut the red tape and come to the immediate aid of those escaping in desperation. When the plague had ravaged Ahmedabad decades ago and most others had fled, he had stayed on, refusing to move out for personal safety, and helped others instead. During his long years of imprisonment, despite ill health, he would make tea for inmates and always take good care of others. This was how he had always been.

In his seventies, battling ill health, Sardar Patel was the deputy prime minister of India and served as acting prime minister every time Jawaharlal Nehru travelled out of the country. He was also the home minister, the minister of states, and the minister in charge of Information and Broadcasting. In addition, he was a member of the Partition Council, the Emergency Committee, and half a dozen committees engaged in drafting the Indian Constitution. Despite his hectic schedule, though, he was never too busy to care.

> Patel was loved by colleagues and party workers because he cared for them and took steps to solve their financial or medical problems even before he was approached.

FORMER INDIAN PRIME MINISTER MORARJI DESAI, SPEAKING ABOUT SARDAR PATEL IN 1987

45

SPEAK UP

Face the bully

In the early 1940s, Britain's Prime Minister Winston Churchill argues that the Second World War with Germany is a battle for freedom. Yet, he cannot accept that the people of India and others colonized by Britain are also entitled to freedom. It is only after Churchill loses the election and the Labour Party comes to power that the Indian Independence Act is passed in the British Parliament. After his humiliating defeat, Churchill wants to re-enter the political stage and seeks to make the loss of the Indian Empire an issue to hit back at his political rivals, and in the process, he makes a scathing attack on India.

Reclining in an armchair in pleasant Dehradun after suffering a massive heart attack a few weeks ago, Patel's eyes fell upon an article in *The Hindustan Times.* His pulse began to rise.

'Have you seen this?' he asked his private secretary Shankar, showing him the text of the speech delivered by former British Prime Minister Winston Churchill on 12 December 1948 in the British Parliament. The acclaimed hero of Britain's victory over Germany in the Second World War had declared that abandoning the Raj and handing over India *to the so-called political classes* was like transferring power to *men of straw*, of whom no traces would remain in a few years.

Indians, Churchill had declared, had no capability to govern themselves and would squander away all the good that the British had done for them.

'Men of straw?' Patel fumed, outraged, infuriated and horrified. 'We must reply to this at once,' he said, directing Shankar to outline a befitting reply.

'Must we rush things?' asked Shankar hesitantly. 'A reply to Churchill would need a great deal of thought and an apt choice of words.' Winston Churchill was, after all, one of the finest orators of the day, whose speeches were the stuff of legend.

'You do not need much thought,' scoffed Patel, 'to deal with a thoughtless speech.'

And so the duo began putting together a strong reply to the outrageous speech.

'Mr Churchill is an unashamed imperialist and at a time when imperialism is on its last legs, he is the proverbial last ditcher for whom obstinacy and dogged consistency mean more than reason, imagination or wisdom,' Patel said, calling Churchill's outburst against India and its government 'characteristically ignorant and extremely prejudiced'.

Winston Churchill was a master of rhetoric. His speeches had instilled confidence in the British people during the darkest days of the war and inspired the Allies to rise as one against the Germans. But Patel was not one to be intimidated by legends and laurels of white men steeped in prejudice.

On the one hand, Churchill waxed eloquent about democracy and equality and freedom; on the other, he had no qualms about supporting imperial despots like the Nizam of Hyderabad, whose forces, known as the Razakars, were spreading terror among people. Egged on by Churchill, the Nizam had declared that Hyderabad would be an independent nation and would not be a part of India. A man so duplicitous and dangerous as Churchill could not be allowed to define India or her leaders.

'Mr Churchill's elastic conscience,' thundered Patel, calling out his shocking hypocrisy, 'had an infinite capacity for putting up with wrongs done by his own race to others.'

Filled with disdain for Hindus, Churchill had famously called them 'a beastly people with a beastly religion'. His support for Jinnah was also well known, despite the covert channel of communication the two leaders had established to keep in touch with secret code names and alternate addresses. Accusing Churchill of scuttling every attempt to aid India, Patel listed out the many mischievous and devious ways Churchill had repeatedly worked against India's interests, including playing a key role in engineering Partition.

Almost everyone who knew Patel and had worked with him closely would call him a man of action and not a man of words. But if any occasion demanded the display of his oratorical flair, this was it.

Snubbing Churchill for the drubbing he received at the elections, Patel said the British people had done well by driving him out of office. He added that while the defeat ought to have made Churchill a wiser man, he seemed to have no capacity to learn or unlearn anything.

'The fact of the matter is,' Patel blasted on, 'whether Mr Churchill roars like a lion or coos like a dove, it is his ignorance and blind prejudice that must come out prominently.'

Warning others not to be misled by such old-world ideas if they wished to have better relations with India, Patel concluded, 'It is only in this spirit and not on the malice and venom of Mr Churchill's tongue that an enduring relationship of friendship, cooperation and collaboration can be built between India and Britain and other members of the Commonwealth.'

After Patel had finalized the stinker, he asked Shankar to dictate it to A.S. Iyengar, the principal information officer of the Government of India in Delhi. 'Ask him to repeat it back so there is no mistake in transcribing it,' said Patel.

'Sardar,' Shankar said from the phone, 'Mr Iyengar is asking...in view of it being about Mr Churchill, does he need to show the letter to Prime Minister Nehru before having it published?'

'No...' Patel shot down the thought, knowing that Nehru would instinctively pick the path of conciliation and not confrontation. 'If it is shown to Jawahar, the reply will never go out at all.'

Patel's stinging response appeared in the newspapers the following day. Predictably, Nehru was annoyed, as was Mountbatten. Even V.P. Menon expressed his anger about not being consulted. But an overwhelming number of people who called Patel after reading the papers offered their heartfelt congratulations to him for taking such a bold stand and speaking up for India.

Ironically, a year later, when Churchill's deputy Anthony Eden visited India, he met Patel. 'I have a message to give you from Mr Churchill,' he said. 'He wanted me to tell you that he read your reply to his speech and thoroughly enjoyed the retort. He says he has nothing but admiration for the manner in which India seems to have settled down. And he also wanted me to convey,' said Eden, 'that he hopes the world will get to see more of Sardar.'

> Power of the pen and of the tongue have to be used with the utmost discretion and a full sense of public duty.

SARDAR PATEL, IN A SPEECH DELIVERED IN HYDERABAD IN 1950

46

NO GRUDGES

Be magnanimous; choose grace

In early 1947, Nawab Hamidullah of Bhopal is the chancellor of the Chamber of Princes, a body representing about six hundred princely kingdoms across the subcontinent. Conveying that he abhors the Congress, the Nawab states that he wants nothing to do with a Congress-dominated India after Independence. Determined to stay out, he tries persuading other rulers to also keep out and either form a third country called Princestan or even consider joining Pakistan. The Nawab's actions collide head-on with Patel's mission of integrating the princely states into India.

Nawab Hamidullah tugged at his waistcoat. A man of letters, he had no problem finding the right words to convey his thoughts on most days. But this was an awkward moment.

After resisting the Congress, spurning its leaders and attempting every trick in the book to keep out of India, here he was – surrendering his rights to India after battling a gamut of emotions. Despite his repeated attempts to foil Patel's dream of unifying the states, Sardar had been nothing but kind to him – even going out of his way to accommodate him and allowing him a short extension that no other state had received.

'I am most grateful for the extension'—Nawab Hamidullah took Sardar's hand in his. 'Now that the decision has been made, I will abide by it faithfully,' he said sincerely. 'I won't disguise the fact that when the fight was on, I used every means to preserve the independence of my state. But now that I have conceded defeat, I hope you will find that I can be as staunch a friend as I was an opponent.'

'Quite candidly'—Sardar patted Nawab Hamidullah, his vision broader than a narrow win-loss lens—'I do not look upon your accession to India as a victory for us or a defeat for you. It is only right and propriety which have triumphed in the end, and, in that triumph, you and I have played our respective roles.'

Sardar, of course, was only being gracious; he hadn't forgotten all that Hamidullah had done over the last few months. Articulate and persuasive, the Nawab of Bhopal had tried his utmost to influence other rulers to keep out of India. But Patel was willing to let go of the past in the interest of a better future.

'I hesitated to join India because I was fearful.' The Nawab looked down at his shoes. 'I had ambitions to play a big role in the Muslim world in the future...and I feared that if I joined India, Mr Jinnah would denounce me as a traitor to the Muslim cause.'

Sardar nodded understandingly. Despite being in opposing camps, he was aware that the Nawab had been under pressure. He knew that the ruler of Bhopal had even considered stepping down from his throne and passing the crown to his eldest daughter, Abida Sultan, leaving the difficult decision to her.

'Sardar, I have no ill feelings towards anyone,' clarified the Nawab. Despite leaning towards the Muslim League in the tumultuous months leading up to Independence, he had been an impartial ruler all along, celebrating both Holi and Eid with the same fervour in his palace. Besides, he had been a nationalist in his younger days, constantly pressing for progress and reform. 'You will find in me a loyal and faithful ally,' he assured Patel.

Giving credit to the Nawab for his honesty and his courage, Patel shook hands warmly with him. 'I value this assurance of friendship.'

On Sardar's part, this warmth was genuine and not just a formality, as would become apparent in his gestures over the next few months. In October 1947, a concerned Nawab Hamidullah contacted Sardar with an urgent telegram regarding his second daughter, Sajida Sultan, who was married to the Nawab of Pataudi.

> CONDITIONS IN PATAUDI STATE ARE AGAIN DETERIORATING AND MY DAUGHTER AND FAMILY HAVE BEEN BROUGHT TO DELHI AND ARE THERE WITH A SICK CHILD.

After making suitable enquiries, Sardar responded promptly with an immediate update on the child's illness.

SHE IS BEING EXAMINED BY DOCTORS AND WILL BE X-RAYED AND AS SOON AS SHE IS IN A POSITION TO LEAVE, I WILL ARRANGE FOR AEROPLANE FOR BHOPAL...YOU NEED HAVE NO ANXIETY.

The Nawab replied, saying how deeply touched and grateful he was for the personal interest and trouble Sardar had taken to look after his daughter and her family.

A few days later, Sardar personally toured the princely state of Pataudi to take stock of the troubles there and updated the Nawab of Bhopal. Despite the rocky history of their relationship and Nawab Hamidullah's repeated efforts to thwart Patel's attempts at unifying India, Sardar was not just saying with words but displaying through action that with those extending a friendly hand to India, he was most willing to bury the unpleasant past, give credit where it was due and move on. Holding grudges had no place in his world.

> "Here is the man whom I once hated. Here is the man whom I later feared. Here is the man whom I now admire and love."

MAHARAJA JIVAJI RAO SCINDIA, ERSTWHILE RULER OF GWALIOR, ABOUT SARDAR PATEL

47

BREAK THE CHAIN OF REVENGE

{ Payback does no good to anybody }

At the end of September 1947, Patel receives a report that a plan is in the offing to attack and block convoys of refugees passing through the city on their way to Pakistan. As India's home minister, the responsibility for the safe passage of those leaving for Pakistan falls upon Patel's shoulders. He rushes from Delhi to Amritsar to tackle the problem head-on.

Closing the file containing the daily report card from Punjab, Patel sat back and shut his eyes. Millions were being ground to dust in the gut-wrenching violence following the Partition of India. People had lost everything – their loved ones, their honour, their home, their land and their sacred shrines. And now they were thirsting for revenge.

The report about the planned attack pained him. This was not how things had been. Hindus, Muslims and Sikhs had lived together in harmony in Punjab for centuries – until one political party – Jinnah's Muslim League – had poisoned that atmosphere of brotherhood and whipped up a communal frenzy with its daily propaganda. *Had they fought all their lives for this kind of freedom, where Indians would butcher one another to death? There would always be matters of difference among people, but were there not so many things that united them as well?*

Determined not to allow the venom to spread any further, Patel decided to make an impromptu dash to Amritsar – to do his best to put an end to the vicious cycle of hatred and revenge.

'I have come to you with a specific appeal,' he pleaded before a group of Sikh leaders who had gathered together urgently in Amritsar after he had rushed there from Delhi, 'to throw in your weight for the maintenance of peace and to pledge the safety of Muslim refugees crossing the city.'

The maharaja of Patiala and other Sikh rulers in the room stared glumly at the floor. Over the past few weeks, thousands of refugees had poured into their kingdoms from west Punjab, which was now in Pakistan. They had come carrying few possessions but bearing many tales of horror.

'I feel it is a disgrace to all that military force should be used to compel them to give transit facilities,' Patel continued. 'Instead, I think it is in keeping with your dignity, reputation and valour that you should raise a volunteer force to guarantee the refugees complete immunity from attacks.'

The rulers and leaders of Punjab exchanged uneasy glances, seeing the wisdom in Patel's words but also knowing the practical difficulty in holding back the angered people.

The ring of revenge and hatred could go on endlessly. And no good could ever come of that. Advocating a workable path, Patel appealed to them, saying, 'Let's break the vicious cycle of attacks in retaliation at least for a week… If the Pakistanis do not respond satisfactorily, India will then take them to task.'

Responding to Sardar's heartfelt plea, the leaders promised to do their best to see that the caravans with Muslims wanting to go to Pakistan could pass through Amritsar safely. This was not, after all, the first time Patel had made urgent appeals for peace. Despite suffering several ailments, he had been travelling relentlessly to deliver his message. 'India has made a tremendous sacrifice for freedom,' he had stressed in speech after speech across the country. 'A part of living India has been torn away. The rest must be whole… Every Indian must now forget that he is Rajput, Jat, Sikh… The watchword of India should be unity… We stand or fall together.'

Assured of support from the Sikh leaders, a relieved Patel decided to return to Delhi. But on his way to the airfield, his car was stopped. People began gathering around. Tired and angry, these were Sikh and Hindu refugees from west Punjab who had fled their homes, trudging great distances on foot through storm and rain, clutching on to their children and meagre belongings. Surrounding his vehicle, they demanded an answer.

Maniben, Sardar's daughter, held her breath. The crowd outside was swelling fast. Hundreds were standing around on all sides, some beating the bonnet, others thumping the trunk. They were all demanding answers from Sardar.

'Let's say we need to get to the airport before dark to return to Delhi,' suggested Patel's private secretary Shankar, sensing blood in the eyes of the crowd outside.

'No.' Sardar shot down the suggestion at once and opened the door, pained by the pitiable faces all around. 'I must listen to them. I must talk to them...'

Stepping out gingerly behind her father, Maniben scanned the angry faces. *How big was this crowd? Thousands? Tens of thousands? A hundred thousand?* The sight was both dizzying and frightening as they were engulfed by a sea of humanity. But her seventy-three-year-old fearless father had climbed on to higher ground to address the crowd.

AILING AND PAST 70, PATEL STEPS IN TO STOP THE CYCLE OF REVENGE AND ALLOW REFUGEES SAFE PASSAGE DURING PARTITION

'In this same city, the blood of Hindus, Sikhs and Muslims mingled in the bloodbath of Jallianwala Bagh,' he reminded them of the massacre of 1919 when Indians of all faiths had stood as one against the British. 'I am grieved to think that things have come to such a pass... The butchery of innocent and defenceless men, women and children does not behove brave men...'

But the crowds were seething with anger; they would settle for nothing less than retribution.

Sardar requested them to pledge the safety of the refugees crossing over to Pakistan, if only to avoid worsening the plight of the refugees on the other side of the border making their way to India.

The thought of desperate Hindus and Sikhs still in Pakistan, trying to reach India, mellowed the crowd. Yes, they were thirsting for revenge, but it could not come at the cost of their brethren, already battered and suffering.

'It does not become a brave people to perpetuate deeds of brutality on defenceless men, women and children,' said Patel. 'If others cast chivalry and honour to the winds, it does not justify us in debasing ourselves. If we have to fight, we must fight clean. No laws of humanity or war among honourable men permit the murder of people who have sought shelter and protection.'

Despite his advancing age, the late hour and the unplanned nature of this speech, Sardar spoke on for over an hour: reasoning, pleading, explaining, beseeching the crowd to hold back their anger and form a force of volunteers to provide the refugees a safe passage to the frontier.

'We have won our freedom to make our country great and prosperous, not to destroy it... The lives of millions are at stake,' he said, requesting that there be a truce for three months during which both sides could exchange refugees. 'Let us take the initiative and break this vicious circle of attacks and counterattacks.'

After the impassioned appeal Sardar made to the leaders and the impromptu speech directly addressing the people, no convoy of refugees going to Pakistan through the city was attacked. Sardar's speech in Amritsar is said to have turned the tide.

> Evil cannot be met with evil, but with good.
>
> SARDAR PATEL, IN A SPEECH AT PATIALA IN OCTOBER 1947

48

ABILITY OVER ANCESTRY

Courtesy counts

In addition to being the deputy prime minister after Independence, Patel is also the home minister of India. Various matters related to internal security, administration and so on fall under his charge. Working under him as home secretary is H.V.R. Iengar.

Pulling his chair closer to the bed, Home Secretary H.V.R. Iengar leaned in towards his boss, trying to make sense of his barely audible voice. Unwell and weak, Vallabhbhai Patel, home minister of India, was reclined on raised pillows, attending to work from his home. 'As I was saying'—Patel took a deep breath as he discussed a matter the home secretary had brought for his approval.

'Bapu'—Patel's daughter Maniben burst into the bedroom—'the maharaja of Patiala is here to meet you.'

'Now?' Patel looked up at his personal secretary. 'Did he have an appointment?'

'Uh…I don't think so…' said Vishnu Shankar, glancing at the clock on the wall, then at his diary.

'He says he was visiting Delhi and decided to drop in as he heard you were unwell,' explained Maniben.

'Hmm…I see…'

Taking the cue, Iengar closed the file in his hand. 'Sir…I will wait till you finish speaking to the maharaja.'

'Where are you going?' asked Patel.

'I'll wait outside.' Iengar excused himself as he rose from his chair. He was, after all, a government official, and the maharaja a royal. Besides, Maharaja Yadavindra Singh was also the Rajapramukh or head of the newly formed union of Punjab States. 'The maharaja is here to meet you…'

'So what? It is to you that I have given an appointment'—Patel gestured for him to sit back down—'not to the maharaja. Please sit down.'

'Call the Maharaja in and ask him to wait,' Patel instructed his daughter. 'Tell him I am in a meeting.'

A few moments later, Mani entered the room, followed by the tall and imposing maharaja of Patiala, a diamond necklace and bejewelled kirpan glittering on his silk tunic.

'Namaste,' Patel greeted him, 'what a pleasant surprise…'

'Apologies for the sudden visit – I heard about your health and couldn't leave Delhi without calling upon you…' said the dashing king, as Iengar stood up to greet him.

'I am happy you came,' said Sardar, accustomed to visitors after he had suffered a heart attack some months ago. 'But I am in the middle of something and request you to wait…' He pointed to a chair near the window. 'Please sit there until I finish…'

'Uh…sure…carry on…' nodded Maharaja Yadavindra Singh, having been told so already by Maniben.

'Go on,' Patel instructed the home secretary to resume their discussion. Only after he had finished about ten minutes later did Patel turn to speak to the Maharaja.

As Iengar retreated, smiling sheepishly about having kept a maharaja waiting, he could not help recalling how many times Patel had stood up for him in their short span of working together.

The next morning when Iengar came in to meet Patel, he could not keep from expressing his surprise at what had happened. 'Sir'—he held a hand to his heart—'yesterday, you showed me exceptional courtesy. I…I uh…just don't know what to say.'

'Ah…it was nothing,' Patel brushed it off. 'The position of Secretary to the Government of India is an important one. It should be given the respect it deserves.'

> 'He will always remain in my memory, as that paradox – a man of iron will, clear vision and ruthless determination, who was, at heart, kind, gentle and sentimental.'

LORD MOUNTBATTEN

49

RECONSTRUCTION, NOT RETRIBUTION

{ Let bygones be bygones }

By 1948, most of the nearly six hundred princely states across the subcontinent have merged with India, but Hyderabad, the largest state, is still holding out. From repeated breakdowns in talks to increasing unrest and violence, Hyderabad appears to be slipping dangerously out of hand. The Government of India then decides to send in the Army to take control of the state. In February 1949, a few months after the ruler of Hyderabad surrenders, Sardar Patel goes to meet him to decide the future course of action.

Holding a hand over his eyes to shield them from the sun's glare, Patel peered out of the plane window, catching his first glimpse of the Nizam of Hyderabad. Sir Mir Osman Ali Khan, the world's richest man, whose dynasty had ruled Hyderabad for over two centuries, was waiting to receive Patel after Hyderabad's surrender to India.

As the plane came to a halt, Sardar unbuckled his seat belt. From the very start, he had known that Hyderabad was going to be a challenge. From the special preference given to the Nizam by the British, labelling him 'His Exalted Highness, The Faithful Ally' and whatnot, to the secret talks between the Nizam and Muslim League leader Muhammad Ali Jinnah lending matters a communal flavour, it had contained all the ingredients for trouble. But it was a state of critical importance, given Hyderabad's geographical position as a link between the north and south. Had the state slipped out of India's hand, the northern half of the country would have been cut off from its south.

'So,' Sardar chuckled as the plane door was thrown open, 'looks like His Exhausted Highness is here!'

'Hmm...' Shankar, Sardar's secretary, made his way to the top of the steps. Below, the Nizam was approaching the plane – a frail figure dressed in a stained and faded achkan. 'I heard he's addicted to opium,' Shankar whispered into Sardar's ear. He would learn later that the Nizam had in fact taken a double dose to sustain himself through the meeting with Patel.

Fingers gripping the handrail, Patel descended the steps, a look of triumph pinned upon his face. Exactly a year ago, India had been discussing compromise schemes with the Nizam's delegation, including terms allowing for the semi-independence of Hyderabad. The Nizam had refused to be treated on par with the other princely states. The chief of his militia, Kasim Razvi, had threatened to conquer the whole of India, to bury Nehru and Sardar in their graves, and to fly the Nizam's flag from the Red Fort in Delhi. After all that false bravado, Hyderabad had fallen to the Indian Army like a pack of cards in less than a week.

Past events buzzing in his head, Sardar stepped on the tarmac. The Nizam, ready to receive him at the foot of the stairway, joined his trembling hands together in salutation, his head slightly bowed, his eyes downcast. Behind Patel, Shankar swallowed hard, feeling a tad sorry for the old man, who had ruled the kingdom for nearly four decades.

'Welcome to Hyderabad,' said the Nizam, his voice soft.

'I'm very happy to be here,' Sardar greeted the Nizam with a smile. 'Tell me, how is your health?'

Shankar exhaled hard as the tension in the air dissolved somewhat in the warmth of Patel's voice. Despite all that had happened in the last year, Sardar displayed no coldness.

Greetings exchanged and courtesies completed, Patel visited the Nizam later at his palace, King Kothi, accompanied by General Chaudhuri, who had led the Army operation for India. Once again, the Nizam personally received Sardar at the portico of his palace and then led them in.

Seated along a semicircular bench, they engaged in small talk over matters like health and the weather for some time, during which Patel's hawk eyes scanned the Nizam, looking for some signs of remorse. Finding none, he decided to lay it out honestly.

'Events of the past year have cast a shadow all over the country,' Patel began. 'Despite every effort from our side to reach a settlement – we even offered Hyderabad special terms – you managed to stonewall us.'

The Nizam shifted uneasily on his seat, pinning his eyes on the ebony centrepiece in the room. On 11 June 1947, he had triumphantly issued a *firman,* declaring that on 15 August 1947, Hyderabad would become an independent and sovereign nation. And here he was, less than two years hence, tying his destiny to India's.

'The Razakar militia under Kasim Razvi were spewing venom on the streets'—Sardar laid the facts out bluntly—'but your administration failed to deal with them. In fact, you supported and encouraged them.'

Over the past years, the Congress party had been banned in the state; over 10,000 of its members had been thrown into jail. About 2,00,000 Razakars with firearms were allowed to roam the streets, leading to widespread fear among the populace. In addition, the communists had spread a reign of terror in large parts and established a parallel government. Arms had been smuggled in from Iran and Pakistan. Law and order had collapsed.

Fidgeting nervously with his fingers, the Nizam pursed his lips. 'I was helpless, you see...helpless against the advice of my Council and the pressure exerted by Razvi and the Razakars.'

'But you also had people giving you sound advice,' argued Patel. 'Your constitutional adviser, Sir Walter Monckton; your former diwan, Sir Sultan Ahmad; and several others. But instead of listening to them, you put your faith in communal voices. You even negotiated with Jinnah and helped Pakistan with a loan!' Patel thrashed out every point, almost as if he were reading out a charge sheet. 'You smuggled in weapons, approached other countries for help, you wrote to British Prime Minister Churchill and to the United Nations.'

Patel was clear that, left to him, the Hyderabad episode would have never reached this stage in the first place. But, at the behest of Menon, the states secretary, and Prime Minister Nehru, he had left it to Viceroy Mountbatten to settle matters in the interest of avoiding yet another confrontation. *After all, wasn't there enough conflict in the country already?* But it had not worked out. Now that he had finally settled it his way, he was certainly not going to brush things under the carpet.

Startled by Sardar's frontal attack, the Nizam stared at his bony fingers. 'I tried my best,' he said hesitantly. 'I was compelled to take these actions. My own life and future were in danger. It was not easy holding the scales between the different groups... I...uh...I was like a prisoner in my own house.'

'Holding the scales even?' Patel scoffed. 'Need I remind you of the fear in which Hindus were living in your state? Of their political subjugation in Hyderabad? And even personally...I believe some of the poems you wrote were grossly communal as well.'

'That...that's not true...' protested a visibly edgy Nizam, who dabbled in composing poetry.

'Shankar'—Sardar turned to his private secretary who had shown Patel the Nizam's composition some months ago—'recite for me that couplet...'

As Shankar hesitantly recited the objectionable verse from the Urdu ghazal that had appeared in a local daily, the

Nizam's face lost all colour. It seemed there was simply no getting away from Sardar's brutal cross-examination. He let out a deep sigh, fearing that the end of his dynasty had come.

'I am willing to let bygones be bygones'—Patel turned to the Nizam, startling him with an olive branch. 'I am willing to ignore the past if there is genuine repentance and remorse...'

The Nizam's face lit up. 'I am sorry.' He folded his hands, jumping at the chance. 'I deeply regret all that happened... believe me...' he pleaded for Sardar's forgiveness. 'I promise you...I give you my word...' he said, sounding most earnest, 'in the future, I will be loyal to India...'

Patel nodded. He was willing to let the past go, provided the other party was also willing to do the same.

'As long as you stand by your word,' said Patel with sincerity, 'you have nothing to fear from the Government of India. We will treat you with courtesy and consideration.'

Blood rushed back to the Nizam's pale face. He took heart in the dramatic change in Patel's attitude. 'I do not know how to thank you for the magnanimity you have shown,' he said, extending his hand, his tone mirroring Patel's sincerity.

The large-heartedness for which the Nizam was expressing gratitude was not reserved for royals alone. Sardar had also extended it to ordinary people. Speaking in Rajkot in November 1947 in the wake of the Partition of India, he had said to the Muslims of Kathiawar who had supported the Muslim League's demand for Pakistan. 'I have forgotten the part which is done and gone...if only you would treat it as such.'

'We wish to heal past wounds and move ahead.' Sardar gripped the Nizam's hand firmly. 'I hope you will walk along. India does not seek revenge or retribution but repair and reconstruction.'

> We cannot, of course, alter what has already happened and it is no use crying over spilt milk. But we must think of the future and find the solution.

SARDAR PATEL, IN A LETTER TO MAHADEV DESAI AFTER COMMUNAL DISTURBANCES IN AHMEDABAD IN APRIL–MAY 1941

50

LETTING GO

Accept the inevitable with grace

It is March 1949; Patel is flying from Delhi to Jaipur for the inauguration of the state of Rajasthan, a complex task that had been accomplished after several months of tough negotiations. Travelling in a mini-aircraft, Sardar is accompanied by his daughter Maniben, his secretary V. Shankar and Maharaja Hanwant Singh of Jodhpur. Due to Sardar's heart condition, the pilot had been instructed not to take the plane higher than 3,000 feet. It is a journey of less than an hour, but on the way, one engine stops functioning, the radio signal dies out and the plane starts losing altitude, slipping slowly into the hills below.

This is not the first time Patel is staring at life's end. From assassination attempts to cancer-fears, he has dodged several near-fatal bullets before, always taking the inevitable prospect of death matter-of-factly in his stride.

LETTING GO
JAIPUR 1948
ON THE WAY FROM DELHI TO JAIPUR
THUDDD!!
CRRCRCCR
RRRRR R R RR
THE UPPER COVER OF THE ENGINE HAS SUDDENLY COME LOOSE. ONE OF THE ENGINES HAS STOPPED!
LOOKS LIKE THIS IS THE END!
CAPTAIN BHIM RAO, THE PLANE IS LOSING ALTITUDE. HOW FAR ARE WE FROM JAIPUR?
WE'RE 30 MILES NORTH OF JAIPUR, YOUR HIGHNESS.

THE PLANE IS LOSING HEIGHT RAPIDLY. WE MUST MAKE AN EMERGENCY LANDING.
BUT WHERE?
LOOK THERE, CAPTAIN! THAT SANDY PATCH ALONG A STREAM MIGHT BE A SUITABLE SPOT.
HMM...EVERYBODY, PLEASE FASTEN YOUR SEAT-BELTS!
IF WE ARE UNABLE TO MAKE A SOFT BELLY LANDING...AND FIND THAT THE GROUND IS ROCKY, THE FUEL TANK MAY CATCH FIRE. OR IT MAY RESULT IN A SHORT-CIRCUIT, WHICH MAY ALSO RESULT IN A FIRE.
IN THAT CASE, THE MAIN DOOR MAY GET JAMMED. THEN, WE WILL NEED TO USE THE EMERGENCY EXIT.

MEANWHILE, THE PLANE GLIDED OVER HILLS AND RAVINES,
UNSTEADILY APPROACHING THE SELECTED SPOT BY A STREAM.
THIS IS THE EMERGENCY EXIT? IT'S SO NARROW!
YES...THIS TWIN-ENGINE RIAF DOVE AIRCRAFT DOES NOT HAVE EMERGENCY EXITS ON THE SIDE, BUT ON THE TOP. WE'LL HAVE TO SQUEEZE OURSELVES OUT...AND WE MUST EVACUATE SWIFTLY.
HOW WILL BAPUJI MANAGE?
UNLIKE THE REST OF THEM, SARDAR WAS IN HIS SEVENTIES, A HEART PATIENT, AND RECOVERING FROM ILLNESS.

THE EXIT MAY NOT BE WIDE, BUT OUR HIGHNESS HERE MOST CERTAINLY IS! IF HE GETS STUCK IN THE EMERGENCY EXIT, THERE WOULD BE NO CHANCE OF ANYONE ELSE GETTING THROUGH!
HA-HA-HA-HA-HA-HA!
SHANKAR'S JOKE FOLLOWED BY SARDAR'S INFECTIOUS LAUGH DISSOLVED THE TENSION IN THE AIR.
A FEW MOMENTS LATER, THE PILOT WAS ABLE TO LAND THE PLANE SAFELY ON THE RIVERBED, WITHOUT INJURIES OR CASUALTIES.
LATER, A VERY ANXIOUS PRIME MINISTER NEHRU GOT ON A CALL WITH PATEL TO ENQUIRE ABOUT THE INCIDENT.
I AM SO GLAD YOU ARE ALRIGHT!
THE PILOT MANAGED IT ALL VERY SMOOTHLY. I ONLY SAT THROUGH A VARIETY OF ENTERTAINMENT!

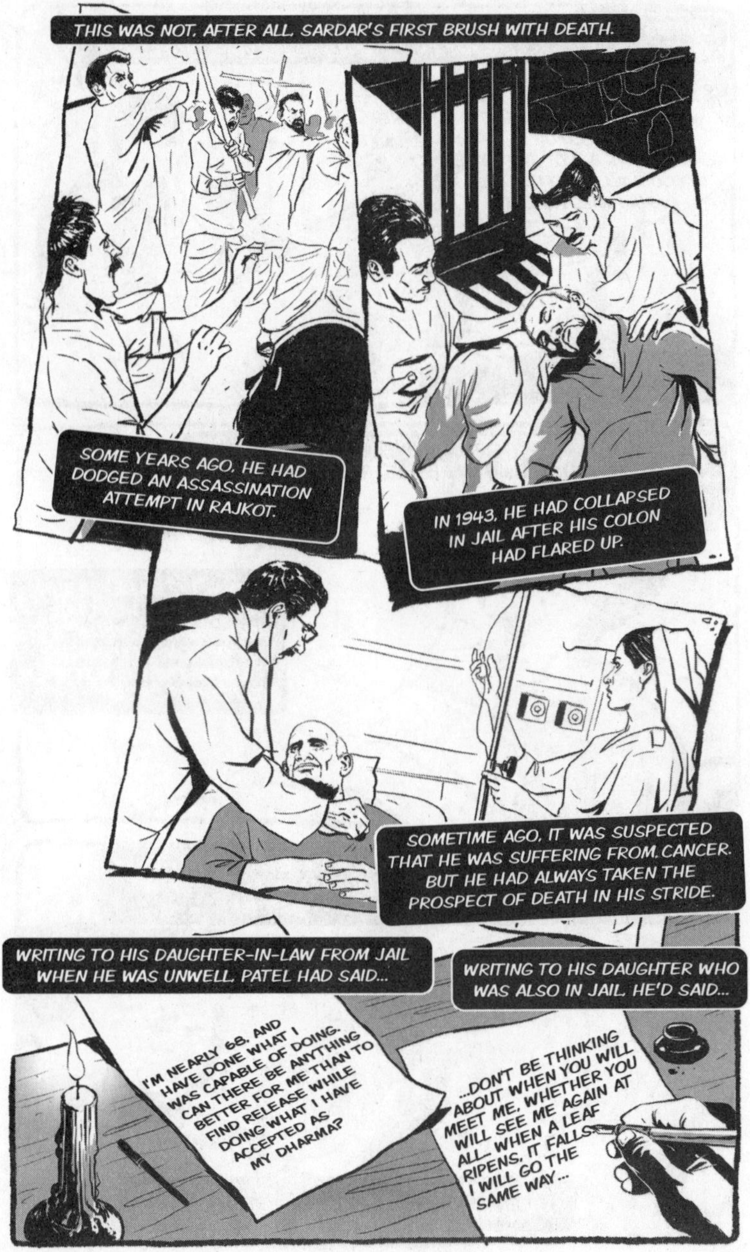
THIS WAS NOT, AFTER ALL, SARDAR'S FIRST BRUSH WITH DEATH.
SOME YEARS AGO, HE HAD DODGED AN ASSASSINATION ATTEMPT IN RAJKOT.
IN 1943, HE HAD COLLAPSED IN JAIL AFTER HIS COLON HAD FLARED UP.
SOMETIME AGO, IT WAS SUSPECTED THAT HE WAS SUFFERING FROM CANCER. BUT HE HAD ALWAYS TAKEN THE PROSPECT OF DEATH IN HIS STRIDE.
WRITING TO HIS DAUGHTER-IN-LAW FROM JAIL WHEN HE WAS UNWELL, PATEL HAD SAID...
I'M NEARLY 68, AND HAVE DONE WHAT I WAS CAPABLE OF DOING. CAN THERE BE ANYTHING BETTER FOR ME THAN TO FIND RELEASE WHILE DOING WHAT I HAVE ACCEPTED AS MY DHARMA?
WRITING TO HIS DAUGHTER WHO WAS ALSO IN JAIL, HE'D SAID...
...DON'T BE THINKING ABOUT WHEN YOU WILL MEET ME, WHETHER YOU WILL SEE ME AGAIN AT ALL. WHEN A LEAF RIPENS, IT FALLS. I WILL GO THE SAME WAY...

WHEN PATEL SUFFERED A HEART ATTACK IN MARCH 1948 A FEW WEEKS AFTER GANDHIJI'S ASSASSINATION, GANDHI'S SON DEVDAS VISITED HIM.
THE ATTACK WAS CAUSED BY THE GRIEF I HAD BOTTLED UP IN MY HEART. BUT IT IS NOT TOO LATE. IF YOU HAVE A LETTER FOR BAPU, I WILL TAKE IT.
TOWARDS THE END OF 1950, WHEN HIS HEALTH WAS FAILING, PATEL SENSED THAT HIS TIME HAD COME.
ZINDAGI KA YEH TAMASHA CHAND ROZ...*
SARDAR OFTEN REPEATED THE LINES OF THE POET NAZIR AS HE MOVED IN AND OUT OF CONSCIOUSNESS – *FUSSING OVER LIFE FOR A FEW SHORT DAYS...
MANY YEARS AGO, PATEL AND GANDHI HAD MADE A PACT – THEY WERE NOT TO LEAVE THIS WORLD TILL INDIA HAD ATTAINED SWARAJYA, AND ONCE THAT HAD HAPPENED, THEY WOULD GO TOGETHER.
MANGAL MANDIR KHOLO, DAYAMAY*...
IT HAD BEEN THREE YEARS SINCE FREEDOM HAD COME, AND GANDHI HAD GONE; NOW SARDAR FELT HIS TIME TOO HAD COME.

DAY AND NIGHT, PATEL HUMMED THE BHAJAN HE HAD OFTEN SUNG AT GANDHI'S ASHRAM, AS LIFE DRAINED FROM HIS BODY: *OPEN YOUR BLESSED DOOR, O MERCIFUL LORD.
MANGAL MANDIR KHOLO, DAYAMAY*...
THAT DOOR UP THERE IS NOT GOING TO OPEN SO EASILY FOR YOU, SARDAR. THERE'S NOT ONE OR TWO BUT THREE LOCKS SECURING IT – ME, SHANKAR AND MANIBEN.
DR NATHUBHAI, DON'T GIVE ME THAT. IT MAKES MY STOMACH WORSE. AND EVEN IF THERE ARE TEN LOCKS, I TELL YOU... IT IS TIME FOR THAT DOOR TO SWING OPEN FOR ME.
A WEEK LATER, SARDAR'S REMARKABLE LIFE CAME TO AN END.
HE'D SPENT HIS LAST FEW DAYS HUMMING THE SONG HE HAD ONCE SUNG WITH GANDHI: 'MANGAL MANDIR KHOLO, DAYAMAY...MANGAL MANDIR KHOLO'.

> Whoever is born is to die one day. Why then should one die as a coward and not as a man?

SARDAR PATEL, IN A SPEECH DELIVERED IN 1942 IN KARAMSAD, GUJARAT

THE HELMSMAN

Before flying to Mumbai for Patel's funeral, Prime Minister Nehru gave a statement to Parliament about Patel's passing away: 'At 9.37 this morning… the story of his great life ended. It is a great story, as all of us know, as the whole country knows, and history will record it in many pages and call him the builder and consolidator of the new India. But perhaps to many of us here he will be remembered as a great captain of our forces in the struggle for freedom and as one who gave us sound advice in times of trouble as well as in moments of victory, as a friend and colleague on whom one could invariably rely, as a tower of strength which revived wavering hearts.'

A Note from the Author

My research into the life of Sardar Patel, for a government project I was writing for many years ago, took me to the back lanes of Ahmedabad in my search for his office.

'Is Sardar Patel's office on this road?' I asked a street vendor in the area, which was the way one got about in a pre–Google-Maps world.

'*Kaun* Sardar Patel?' asked a young man.

It left me stunned. Here was a leader who had united India, who had pulled off the impossible by putting a nation together against all odds, who had achieved something unparalleled in the world – and yet, he was not known in his own backyard?

On that day, I resolved to do something. I had no idea what it would be...but I decided I'd do something to make up for this yawning gap in public knowledge about him. I went back and started a blog. I spoke to small groups of children about him whenever I got an opportunity. I also wrote a book about the thrilling saga of accession, titled *565: The Dramatic Story of Unifying India*, also published by Hachette India.

This book is yet another attempt to fulfil a promise I had made to myself.

The stories you read about Patel's life in this book are true. However, some liberties have been taken in shortening lengthy speeches and formal letters to make it simpler for young readers.

History is more than a saga of kings and wars. The past informs the present and determines the future. It is my hope that these stories from the life of Sardar Patel will not only help you know more about India but also hold up a lamp to guide you through life.

Acknowledgements

'That it was going to be Sardar's 150th birth anniversary in 2025 occurred to me nearly at the end of 2024. Having done extensive research on him, I had so many stories to share about Patel. I had been mulling over the idea of an anecdotal biography of Patel for a while. It seemed befitting to have it out before October 2025. But I wondered – with less than a year to go, and given other writing commitments, was it doable? Absolutely! When a publisher and editor like Vatsala Kaul Banerjee gets behind you, it's always doable! Thanks Vatsala, for taking this on despite the tight deadlines. The thorough fact-checking, editing inputs and complete commitment that a manuscript receives from you is what makes working with you such a pleasure.

I thank Prof. Sunthar at IIT Bombay for signing me on, some years ago, as curator and content writer for the Government of India NVLI portal about Sardar Patel. That is what set me off on this journey and, much like Alice in

Wonderland, I too have been falling deeper and deeper into this rabbit hole. My research led me to writing *565: The Dramatic Story of Unifying India* (also published by Hachette India, in 2024), and now to this book. Thank you for flagging it all off.

Many thanks to Mohit Suneja, for bringing the stories alive with his engaging visuals and vibrant comics. Helping young readers find meaning and purpose in history is often challenging; Mohit's artwork goes a long way in making it easier.

My late Tatha, to whom this book is dedicated – I am indebted to him for sharing stories about the freedom struggle, as he had witnessed them. Very early on, it sparked in me curiosity about the past and a love for history, which has remained a constant.

And as always, gratitude beyond words can ever express to my parents, my husband Shashi and my children, for their unwavering support and love.